Good Kids,
Tough Choices

Also by Rushworth M. Kidder

The Ethics Recession: Reflections on the Moral Underpinnings of the Current Economic Crisis

Moral Courage: Taking Action When Your Values Are Put to the Test

How Good People Make Tough Choices: Resolving the Dilemmas of Ethical Living

Shared Values for a Troubled World: Conversations with Men and Women of Conscience

Heartland Ethics: Voices from the American Midwest (editor)

In the Backyards of Our Lives

Reinventing the Future: Global Goals for the 21st Century

An Agenda for the 21st Century

E. E. Cummings: An Introduction to the Poetry

Dylan Thomas: The Country of the Spirit

Good Kids, Tough Choices

How Parents Can Help Their Children Do the Right Thing

Rushworth M. Kidder

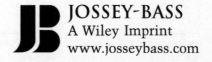
JOSSEY-BASS
A Wiley Imprint
www.josseybass.com

Published by Jossey-Bass
A Wiley Imprint
989 Market Street, San Francisco, CA 94103-1741—www.josseybass.com

Readers should be aware that Internet Web sites offered as citations and/or sources for further information may have changed or disappeared between the time this was written and when it is read.

Limit of Liability/Disclaimer of Warranty: While the publisher and author have used their best efforts in preparing this book, they make no representations or warranties with respect to the accuracy or completeness of the contents of this book and specifically disclaim any implied warranties of merchantability or fitness for a particular purpose. No warranty may be created or extended by sales representatives or written sales materials. The advice and strategies contained herein may not be suitable for your situation. You should consult with a professional where appropriate. Neither the publisher nor author shall be liable for any loss of profit or any other commercial damages, including but not limited to special, incidental, consequential, or other damages.

Jossey-Bass books and products are available through most bookstores. To contact Jossey-Bass directly call our Customer Care Department within the U.S. at 800-956-7739, outside the U.S. at 317-572-3986, or fax 317-572-4002.

Jossey-Bass also publishes its books in a variety of electronic formats. Some content that appears in print may not be available in electronic books.

Library of Congress Cataloging-in-Publication Data

Kidder, Rushworth M.
  Good kids, tough choices : how parents can help their children do the right thing / Rushworth M. Kidder.
    p. cm.
  Includes bibliographical references and index.
  ISBN 978-0-470-54762-5 (pbk.); ISBN 978-0-470-87551-3 (ebk); ISBN 978-0-470-87552-0 (ebk); ISBN 978-0-470-87553-7 (ebk)
  1. Parenting. 2. Child psychology. 3. Parent and child. 4. Child rearing. 5. Decision making–Moral and ethical aspects. I. Title.
  HQ755.8.K53 2010
  649'.64—dc22

                                                                2010021304

Printed in the United States of America
FIRST EDITION
PB Printing   10 9 8 7 6 5 4 3 2 1

Contents

For my wife and daughters, the ever-fixéd marks

Acknowledgments

This book was launched by a comment from a wise and wonderful philanthropist in California, Louise Greeley. "Why don't you do a book on ethics for parents?" she said to me one day.

Through a lifetime of promoting important causes, she'd come to understand that our collective global future lies in raising children of integrity. She was familiar with the conceptual frameworks we had developed at the Institute for Global Ethics around shared values, ethical decisions, and moral courage. But she'd also observed that many parents, facing ethical issues with their children and not knowing what to say, either come at their kids with moral sledgehammers or tiptoe past on eggshells. She saw the need for helping parents teach their children what she called the "habits of obedience" to moral principles, through which kids learn how to work their way courageously through life's toughest decisions.

When it came time to convene workshops and interview parents to gather information for this book, we received further significant support from the Isabel Foundation in Flint, Michigan, and from Betty Barker, a dedicated member of the Institute for Global Ethics' board of directors. We've also had strong financial support from other institute members, including John and Zemula Fleming, Larry Mills, Helmer Ekstrom, Jayne I. Hanlin, Jennifer B. Dyck, Judith A. Stauder, and Nancy Farmer-Martin.

This work would never have taken shape without the dedication and hard work of Polly Jones, my executive assistant at the institute, and Lynda Sleight, who devoted months to finding and interviewing the parents whose real-life narratives form the backbone of this book. My colleagues at the Institute all had a hand in shaping and sustaining this work as well, including Graham Phaup, Marty Taylor, Paula Mirk, Sheila Bloom, Marilyn Gondek, Amber Kruk, Linda Leach, Marie Demmons, Andrea Curtis, and Pat Smith. In addition, I owe great thanks to my literary agent, Rafe Sagalyn, whose clarity helped shape the initial outline, and to my editors at Jossey-Bass, Alan Rinzler and Nana K. Twumasi, who gently brought the book to its final form.

But no one has had more to do with this book, word by word, than my wife, Liz. In ways large and small, her influence has been pervasive, from decades of conversations about ethics and parenting to scores of comments penciled in the margins of manuscripts. Finally, I could never have written it without the experience of being a parent to our two extraordinary daughters. From these three family members, I continue to learn the real meaning of ethics, and it is to them that I dedicate this book.

Lincolnville, Maine
June 2010

Good Kids, Tough Choices

Introduction: Three Lenses for Ethical Parenting

W hat do parents really want for their kids? Call it *character*, *integrity*, *virtue*, *morality*, or *ethics*—whatever term you use, it comes down to living a values-based life. Yes, parents want children who are bright and intelligent, who find success and achievement, who are content with themselves and happy with others. But in a deep and essential way, parents long to raise *good kids*. In other words, they want children who know how to do three things: live by sound guidelines, arrive at wise decisions, and have the courage of their convictions. Put another way, they want children capable of knowing what's right, making tough choices, and standing for conscience.

This book is about these three things. We call them *lenses*— ways of looking at the world to magnify the goodness, spot the pitfalls, and show the way forward. The first of these concepts— knowing what's right—helps you and your children focus on the five shared moral values that are common to cultures around the world: honesty, responsibility, respect, fairness, and compassion. Turn this lens around, and it defines unethical behavior. What's unethical is whatever is dishonest, irresponsible, disrespectful, unfair, or lacking in compassion. As a parent, what do you do when your small-framed thirteen year old tells you his best friend's mom took the two of them to the movies, told the box office he was eleven, and bought him a twelve-and-under child's ticket? To him, she was being irresponsible, even dishonest. But she may have seen it as thrifty, even clever. What should he do the next time that happens? In a world that's losing the ability to choose right over wrong, the knowing-what's-right lens is an essential tool.

But what happens when two deeply held values come into conflict with each other? The second lens, making tough choices, helps you see that the world's hardest calls are about right versus right, not right versus wrong. What do you do when loyalty pulls you one way but truth telling pulls you another, or when what's good for your child is bad for the group? How do you respond when justice comes down on one side and mercy on the other, or when short-term needs are pitted against long-term requirements? Our toughest dilemmas arise when these four patterns emerge. In our shorthand, we call them *paradigms* and label them as truth versus loyalty, individual versus community, justice versus mercy, and short term versus long term. Suppose your daughter, who stars on her high school basketball team, assures you she's kept up with her homework despite frequent long road trips. But the day of the play-offs, just as she's leaving home for the game, a letter arrives from the school saying she's failing all her courses. You want to confront her *this instant*—although that could wreck the game for everyone. Your wife urges you to wait until later, even though that might diminish the seriousness of the matter in your daughter's eyes. In this short-term-versus-long-term dilemma, what do you do when you and your wife are each right but you can't do both things at once? The making-tough-choices lens gives you and your children a framework for addressing life's difficult decisions.

There will be times, however, when the choice is crystal clear but nobody dares to carry it out. The third lens, standing for conscience, illuminates the moral courage you need in order to take action when your values are put to the test. Moral courage lets you face down the challenges arising from fear, cowardice, or ambiguity. It helps you overcome a desire to flee, duck, waffle, or appease. It gives you the confidence to confront and stand firm. How do you counsel your spindly eight-year-old musician after he's seen a popular class athlete cheating on a test where a high score would disadvantage others in the class? Somebody needs to speak up to the teacher—but should your son be the one to do it? Given the dangers, will he dare? Given what's at stake, however, how can he not? The standing-for-conscience lens gives you a way to talk to your children about their own bravery, conviction, and resolve.

This book gives you a crisp, practical framework for using these lenses to build what we at the Institute for Global Ethics have branded as Ethical Fitness®—a term so unique and compelling that we've registered it. Like physical fitness, ethical fitness is not an inoculation or a one-off immersion. It's a process that doesn't happen all at once. It grows gradually, gets you in shape, and lets you respond more easily to the tough climbs. And then, like physical fitness, it disappears if you don't persist. Ethical fitness didn't arise solely for this book. I have developed it in two of my previous books, and it has been tested in the crucible of tough decision making through two decades of work at the Institute for Global Ethics. We've hammered it out with tens of thousands of participants in corporations, schools, nonprofits, military organizations, and government agencies in the United States and overseas. We're now taking these well-seasoned ideas to one of the most important audiences we'll ever reach: parents, who, more than any other group, will determine the ethical fitness of the coming generation.

How to Use This Book

This book applies these three lenses of values, decisions, and courage to scores of real-life stories that parents have told us in interviews over the past several years. There's nothing inflated, abstract, or glamorized about these stories. Unlike some scenarios used in ethics classrooms, these narratives are personal and authentic. They don't pose agonizing choices about whether to switch a trolley that's about to kill five people onto a side track where it will only kill one, or which person to toss out of a sinking lifeboat so the rest will survive, or whether to take multiple organs from one child so that four others can live. Such stories leave the impression that ethical dilemmas are catastrophic events totally apart from ordinary life. Frankly we've never met a single parent or child who has faced such a dilemma, so we don't use them here. Given a choice of having readers say, "That's a sensational story!" or, "That's exactly what's happened to me!" we unhesitatingly choose the latter.

This book, then, is about the common challenges that parents face in the daily, hourly, practical work of raising good kids. It focuses on the interface where parents and children personally encounter ethical challenges and have to find their way through. That's why we avoid sound-bite ethics—those condensations that try to compress wrenching dilemmas into two sentences. Although a few summaries appear in the book, the chapters center on extended narratives because that's how we heard these stories in our interviews. Moral judgments are often shaped by details, and we've learned in our workshops that bare-bones summaries invite snap judgments that misrepresent the way parents really work through dilemmas with their kids. In fact, but for space limitations, we'd provide novel-length treatments of each story, so that readers could get to know these characters in something like the way these characters know each other in real life.

In presenting these stories, we have generally changed names to protect the privacy of the families they describe. Unless otherwise noted, however, the words in quotation marks are exactly as we heard them from our sources. Many of these stories were initially told to my research assistant, Lynda Sleight, who, tape recorder in hand, vigorously sought out parenting stories. Others came to us during seminars or in interviews I conducted. Although our interviews spanned a range of religions and races, they all took place within the United States. We have no doubt that many of our findings have global applications, but because parenting reflects and draws from the culture in which it happens, it seemed best to leave international examples for future books.

In an effort to make this a thoroughly useful book, the five central chapters are organized by age, from birth through age twenty-three. But they're also arranged more loosely around our three lenses of knowing what's right, making tough choices, and standing for conscience. Since these ideas seem to come to light progressively as children develop, the chapters begin with a tight focus on core values (lens 1), move into decision making in the middle years (lens 2), and shift to considerations of moral courage (lens 3) in the older age groups. But since the chapters are collections of stories and since human stories are vigorous, unruly things that don't conform neatly to such packages, quite often all three lenses appear in a single narrative, for which we make no apologies. Nor do we apologize for occasionally reexplaining our frameworks in succeeding chapters. We suspect many parents who pick up this book will have an age-specific interest and will plunge into a particular chapter without reading the preceding material. That's fine. For their sake, we've added a glossary at the end to help them grasp the ethical constructs we're using. But it does mean that those who read straight through may notice some modest and pardonable (we hope) repetition.

The first of these central chapters, spanning birth through age four (Chapter Two), is largely focused on the first lens. Here, the need for the very youngest children to master the core values and begin to distinguish right from wrong is paramount. By ages five through nine (Chapter Three), children who are still absorbing the values are also beginning to sense the need for our second lens: making tough choices. By ages ten through fourteen (Chapter Four), the decision-making processes are in full ascendency, but moral courage (our third lens) is also peeking around the corner. By ages fifteen through eighteen (Chapter Five), children become increasingly independent actors, and moral courage and decision making become the major focus.

While a book on parenting could be excused for stopping at age eighteen, we've added a chapter focused on young adults, ages nineteen through twenty-three (Chapter Six). That's because, at this age, our second and third lenses of ethical reasoning and moral courage are continuing to develop strongly—and not a moment too soon! As these young adults have moved on from adolescence, they have suddenly found that they can legally drive, vote, drink, enlist, and form intimate relationships with the opposite sex. Some are moving from the structured high school years to the more organic openness of university life, while others are shifting from the casual commitments of part-time work to the responsibilities of full-time employment. These changes raise significant new ethical challenges—many of which happen while surprising numbers of these young adults are still living under the parental roof or have returned home for economic reasons.

What If I Face Ethical Dilemmas of My Own?

Coping with these changes raises moral dilemmas for parents as well as for their children. One constant throughout these chapters, in fact, is the concern parents expressed about the ethical challenges they themselves encounter. To be sure, a lot of ethical parenting focuses on dilemmas that their children face. But parents are also thrust into moral conundrums of their own—for no other reason than that they happen to be parents. One interviewee told me how she wrestled over whether to hire a wonderful nanny who insisted on being paid only in cash, off the books, to avoid taxes—a parenting dilemma that happened before she was even a parent! At the other end of the scale, we've included in Chapter Six a harrowing tale from a woman who faced ongoing ethical challenges even after her daughter finally left home for good in her early thirties.

But perhaps what most unites these chapters is a refrain we kept hearing from the parents we interviewed: doubt. When it comes to helping children grasp core values, make ethical decisions, and develop character-building courage, parents today are often spooked. They don't feel they know what to say without sounding preachy, or old-fashioned, or simply naive. Too often they end up saying nothing. That's not only a shame, it's unnecessary. As we listened to scores of parents telling us their tales, we were surprised and delighted by the principled, well-reasoned, and even daring ethical approaches they took. Parents need encouragement, frameworks, and vocabularies for discussion, all of which this book seeks to provide. And their looming, troubling question—"Am I really a good parent?"—needs to be rephrased into a more practical and useful query: "How can I become a better parent?" In the realm of ethics—take it from us—today's parents generally have a lot to build on. They aren't starting at square one. At the very least, they want to raise children of character, and they're committed to doing so if they possibly can. As in any other field of human endeavor, however, ethical parenting encourages us to build confidence through persistent effort within systematic frameworks. To do that, parents need to know something about the social and moral environment their children are facing. That's why we begin the book by looking at three significant pieces of research—about lying preschoolers, media-marinated teens, and college kids wearing fake sunglasses—that help us understand today's parent-child landscape.

1

Raising Kids in Today's Moral Environment

In a small room at a university research center in Kingston, Ontario, a three year old sits quietly in a tiny chair. Above her, hidden in the ceiling, is a video camera. Behind her, out of view, stand a small table and a larger chair. On the table are a few objects covered by a cloth. She's there, so she's been told, to play a game with an adult where she guesses the names of toys by identifying the sounds they make. If she guesses right, she wins a prize.

As the game begins, the adult—actually a trained experimenter—sits on the chair behind the girl and takes a toy from under the cloth, careful to keep it hidden from the child's eyes. If we'd been a fly on the wall, we might have heard a conversation and seen a sequence of events that went something like this:

"What do you hear?" asks the experimenter as she flips the switch on the toy, setting off the unmistakable sound of a siren.

"A police car!" giggles the three year old triumphantly, without turning around to see.

"Right! Good for you!!" responds the experimenter, taking out a second toy and squeezing it.

"To infinity—and beyond!" the toy's deep voice proclaims.

"That's Buzz Lightyear!" says the child, correctly identifying a popular TV Disney character.

"Yes! Wow, you're really good!" exclaims the researcher, who reaches for a third toy. But just then the door opens, and an assistant tells her she has a phone call. She gets up to leave, telling the child that she'll be right back, but that she'll set the next toy on the table and play the sound while she's gone.

"Don't turn around to peek and look at the toy," she says as she crosses the room. "Remember, no peeking."

The door shuts behind her, and the sound begins—a snippet of classical music, utterly unrelated to the toy on the table or to any known toy. As the seconds tick by, the child can stand the suspense no longer. Glancing around hurriedly, she catches sight of a Barney doll on the table and quickly turns back.

A moment later, the knob rattles several times before the door opens. "Remember, don't turn around," the experimenter says as she returns. After covering the Barney doll with the cloth, she asks the child to turn her chair around and face her.

"While I was gone, did you turn your head to the side?" she asks, mimicking the action as she speaks.

"Nuhnt-uh," says the child.

"Did you move around in your chair?"

"No."

"Did you peek to see who it was?"

"No-oh . . . "

"What do you think the toy is?"

"Barney!"

What the Research Tells Us

Conversations like this are all part of a day's work for Victoria Talwar, a leading researcher on children's lying behavior. The response of this child—one of 101 children, aged three to seven, who participated in this experiment—is not surprising: she peeked, and then she lied.

But that isn't what Dr. Talwar wants to know. Her goal is to see how well children dissemble and the age at which they start. Can they cover their tracks well enough to prevent what she calls "semantic leakage," where their words give away their deceptions?

Or do they betray themselves so obviously that a group of students and adults, reviewing the videotapes after these sessions, can readily tell who was lying and who wasn't?

When Does Lying Begin?

In fact, most children (according to the videotapes) peeked. When asked whether they peeked, most children lied, by identifying Barney correctly (and implicating themselves, as did this three year old), feigning ignorance, or pretending to guess another toy. Much of that squares with earlier research. But Dr. Talwar's most important finding—the one that every parent needs to grasp—is more sobering: lying, it seems, is an acquired art, and it develops rapidly in the preschool years (ages three to five), settling in during ages six and seven, and progressing onward from there. Dr. Talwar and her fellow researcher, Kang Lee, are careful not to overstate their findings. In their 2002 paper, they note only that "children under 8 years of age are not fully skilled lie-tellers."[1]

Fully skilled lie tellers. It's a phrase guaranteed to chill the heart of any caring parent. What *is* a fully skilled lie teller? When do children reach that stage? How do they get there? Do they soak up that talent, as some researchers suggest, by watching adults tell everything from white lies to whoppers? Do they lie to protect themselves from punishment, or their friends from exposure, or their parents from aggravation? Do they lie out of fear, or acquisitiveness, or envy, or confusion? Does lying actually signal a sharp, incisive mind, playing across a wide variety of signals, choosing the most likely prevarications, and carefully remembering the results? Or is it a behavior selected by the weaker willed, the rule benders, the morally listless? Finally, do they lie in different ways depending on the importance of the matter at hand? Are children more likely to lie about peeking at a doll than, say, witnessing a robbery? Or do high-stakes events prompt even deeper deception?

Fine questions, those, for academic researchers. But in the kitchen table laboratories of the home, the message for parents is much less complex. There, as in this experiment, age makes all the difference. Most three year olds in Dr. Talwar's lab didn't lie, instead confessing that they had peeked. By contrast, most four to seven year olds did lie. Yet even they haven't yet developed the full panoply of skills that consummate liars need. Those apparently come on in the later years.

The conclusion is that there's a brief window during which children rapidly learn how to lie—and when parents can most effectively intervene.

The implications of that simple statement are enormous. Unless we're content to produce a nation of fully skilled lie tellers, we apparently can't wait until middle or high school to start teaching our children about deception. Nor, given the early age at which this window opens, can we afford to turn the task of honesty building over to teachers, coaches, or caregivers. We've got to hand the task to parents—and parents have got to agree to take it up. The task, simply put, is to help create fully skilled truth tellers.

Controlling the Influence of Electronic Media

But is it enough for parents simply to work on ethics in the early years, assuming they can't do anything after the age of eight? No. Although the effort begins in the prekindergarten years, it doesn't end there. By the age of eight, the target of parental concern shifts to what may well be the most powerful influence in children's lives: the electronic media. Kids from eight to eighteen, according to a survey published in 2010 by the Kaiser Family Foundation, spend an average of seven and a half hours a day with some form of media. That's more time than "in any other activity besides (maybe) sleeping," the researchers note—"almost the amount of time most adults spend at work each day, except that young people use media seven days a week instead of five." Try awakening a teenager in the morning, they write, and "the odds are good that you'll find a cell phone tucked under their pillow—the last thing they touch before falling asleep and the first thing they reach for upon waking."[2]

When you take into account the modern phenomenon of media multitasking—listening to music on an iPod while visiting Facebook, thumbing through a magazine while watching TV, texting a friend while playing a video game—the hours run even higher. The heaviest users turn out to be the so-called tweens—those preteens and early teenagers between eleven and fourteen years old. "The jump in media use that occurs" in this age group, say Kaiser researchers, "is tremendous," ramping up by more than four hours a day from their earlier years. Tweens average nearly nine hours of media exposure a day. But even that number is deceptive: these children actually soak up twelve hours of media content each day, although about three of those hours are accounted for by multitasking. And even that figure underrepresents the total use of media, since the Kaiser survey excluded school-related uses, cell phone calling, and text messaging. Yet just over half of eight to eighteen year olds spend nearly two hours—one hour fifty-six minutes, to be exact—on cell phones each day, and those who also text send an average of 118 messages a day.

How should parents respond? It's easy to tumble into the ain't-it-awful syndrome and write off every encounter with the media as a corrupting and unethical force. But it's well to remember that parents themselves often use media for good purposes. They listen to news on the car radio, watch sporting events and cultural programming on TV, go to movies, and access the Web for everything from planning trips to settling dinner table debates. Still, the Kaiser report sets off serious alarm bells about the moral impact of media use. It finds that heavy users of media—the one-fifth of all kids who consume more than sixteen hours of media content in a single day—get lower grades in school and report lower levels of personal contentment. The research can't tell us whether kids get lower grades and feel more discontented because they immerse themselves in media, or whether they seek solace in media because they feel unhappy and can't hack the schoolwork. Either way, however, there's a serious problem here. If parents have a moral obligation to raise children to do their best and be personally contented, it's hard to avoid the conclusion that where media and children connect, the lighter the better.

Can parents influence this interface? Indeed they can. Children raised in homes where parents leave the TV on in the background all day (45 percent of all households) or turn it on during meal-times (64 percent of all households) become much heavier TV watchers than other children—as do children whose parents let them have TVs in their bedrooms. Parents, then, can provide an atmosphere in the home where media are present but not intrusive. They can also set rules for media use in terms of both content and total time allowed. Setting such limits probably affects children's performance in school, since nearly one-third of all children report that they try to multitask while doing their homework. Conclusion? "Kids whose parents *don't* put a TV in their bedroom," write the Kaiser researchers, *"don't* leave the TV on during meals or in the background when no one is watching, or *do* impose some type of media-related rules spend substantially less time with media than do children with more media-lenient parents."[3]

Media-lenient parents. The phrase, like *fully skilled lie tellers*, sends a shiver down the parental spine—in part because becoming "media lenient" is so easy to do. Parents don't necessarily think of the media as conditioners of life or forces for good or bad. Media are just . . . well, *there*. Like a morning drizzle or the sound of distant traffic, media are a fact of life—a mild annoyance at times and a slight comfort at others, but nothing you can do much about. Or so it seems. Yet the willingness of young people to marinate themselves increasingly in media—from seven and a half hours of total daily media exposure in 1999 to ten hours in 2009—suggests that parents have a positive moral obligation to help them recognize and resist the stuff they're soaking up.

The ethical downsides of this immersion are obvious. The video-gaming fourteen year old who shrinks inward and loses real human contact with other boys; the tween who sends a nude video clip of herself via cell phone to a friend and finds it lodged forever on YouTube; the heavy TV user who searches out ever more violent and abusive programming to satisfy his thirst for excitement; the texting teenage driver who kills himself and others on the highway—all of these raise enormous ethical questions and cry out for a moral response. But Microsoft researcher Linda Stone describes a more subtle challenge. She calls it "continuous partial attention"—the habit, developing steadily in the early teen years, of accessing all sorts of media inputs at once without giving full attention to any one. Stone distinguishes continuous partial attention from multitasking. The latter, she writes, is "motivated by a desire to be more productive and more efficient. Each activity has the same priority—we eat lunch *and* file papers." Continuous partial attention, by contrast, arises from "a desire not to miss anything. We're engaged in two activities that both demand cognition. . . . We're carrying on a conversation at dinner and texting under the table."[4]

Why does that matter? Because continuous partial attention, she suggests, "demands a kind of vigilance that is not characteristic of multi-tasking." Such behavior "creates an artificial sense of crisis" that can lead to "over-stimulation and lack of fulfillment." In a paradox plaguing those who praise multitasking, Stone notes that "the latest, greatest powerful technologies are now contributing to our feeling increasingly powerless. Researchers are beginning to tell us that we may actually be doing tasks more slowly and poorly."

As kids move into this world of complex cognitive multitasking, it's not surprising that parents resort to the complaint that has become almost a mantra in some households: "You're not paying attention!" In fact, the problem is quite the opposite: the child is paying too much attention to all sorts of things at once, trained to do so by a media-rich environment that rewards constant electronic monitoring and by a peer culture that penalizes those who are out of the loop. Parents willing to set rules and shape environments, however, can make a difference. By shifting the home atmosphere from media lenient to media lean, they can have a significant impact on their children.

Helping Children Be Real in a World of Fakes

By the time children escape to college, then, is parenting done? Hardly. Consider, for example, what happened to eighty-five college students at the University of North Carolina the day they were asked to wear counterfeit sunglasses.

When these students—all women—showed up at the university's Center for Decision Research in Chapel Hill, they were told they'd be part of a marketing study evaluating different pairs of sunglasses. They were also told that in addition to receiving their one dollar participant's fee, they could also earn up to twenty-four dollars more during the day. They began their session by looking at pictures of a range of products and answering some questions about them. Some of the products, they were told, were counterfeits, and others were genuine.

The students were then randomly assigned by a computer to two groups. Some were told that because they appeared to have "a relative preference for counterfeit products," they were to go to the room next door and pick up a pair of glasses from a box marked "Counterfeit Sunglasses." Others were asked to pick up their glasses from a box of designer eyewear made by Chloe, valued at about three hundred dollars a pair. In fact, both boxes contained authentic Chloe glasses: the only difference was that while the first group thought they were wearing counterfeits, the second group understood that they were wearing the real thing.

The groups were then given worksheets, each with twenty matrixes on them that looked something like the one in Figure 1.1. In each matrix, they were asked to find two numbers adding up exactly to ten and mark them on the worksheet. For every matrix they completed, they would get fifty cents. When the bell rang, each woman was asked to write down on a collection slip the

1.69	1.82	2.91
4.67	4.81	3.05
5.82	5.06	4.28
6.36	5.19	4.57

Figure 1.1 Sample Matrix Worksheet

number of matrixes she'd solved, throw away her worksheet in a recycling box, and hand in the slip to the experimenter.

It was a setup, clearly, that invited cheating. Without the accompanying worksheet, who knew how many matrixes a student had really solved? Why not push the self-reported score a little—and make a bit more money? What difference would it make? What the students didn't know was that they hadn't really "thrown away" their worksheets. By analyzing them later, the researchers could readily determine who had cheated and who had not.

You may already have suspected the result. Among those wearing the real sunglasses, 30 percent cheated. Among those wearing fakes, 71 percent cheated. That's an astonishing difference. Put someone into counterfeit eyewear, it appears, and that person's propensity to cheat more than doubles. Summarizing their findings, researchers Francesca Gino, Michael I. Norton, and Dan Ariely conclude that wearing counterfeits signals "an aspiration to be something one is not," generating in those wearers "a feeling of a 'counterfeit self' that leads them to behave unethically."[5]

A *counterfeit self*. Here too the skin tingles. Is this, parents ask, what we've raised? If a child can reach adulthood with a moral compass so unstable that a pair of fake shades can compromise his or her values, what have we been doing? Have we created an environment so devoid of authenticity that kids lose the distinction between the real and fake? Is this what happens when "fully skilled lie tellers" are raised by "media-lenient parents?" Or was the sunglasses experiment skewed? Did the researchers so firmly plant the idea of a "relative preference for counterfeit products" that the students believed they really had such a preference and acted accordingly? No. Further tests with the sunglasses confirmed that the same pattern prevailed even when the wearer was not told she had a preference for fakes, but instead knew that she was being randomly assigned to wear the counterfeits. Conclusion: If you know you're wearing knockoffs, you're more likely to cheat.

Clearly this research isn't about sunglasses. It's not even about fashion in general. It's about the impact on oneself of knowingly participating in fraudulent activity—the sense of what psychologists describe as "self-alienation" versus "authenticity." When people report that they don't feel they know themselves very well or are out of touch with the "real me," they don't feel a sense of authenticity. That, in fact, was the basis of the final task these experimenters performed. The participants were asked to assess themselves through a series of well-tested questions designed to probe self-alienation. Those who answered while wearing fake glasses reported feeling less authentic and more self-alienated than those wearing the real thing.

The lesson for parents? As kids mature, even the most seemingly innocuous activity—dressing in phony designer jeans, sporting the street corner Rolex, carrying the knockoff purse—can have a moral impact. While they may believe, in these researchers' words, that "they are simply getting similar products for less money," in fact they "may be paying a price in terms of their long-term morality." It appears that our outward manifestation of ethics is driven in part by our inward sense of ourselves. Put simply, counterfeit selves do counterfeit things, and fakery breeds more fakery. Parents who long to help their teenagers live lives of healthy integrity understand this intuitively. They know their task is to encourage, demand, and exhibit authenticity—not in piecemeal ways, but with a full recognition that the smallest details add up to life-changing ethical habits. They know that by changing their children's mental sunglasses—encouraging them to look at the world through genuine moral lenses rather than through frauds and fakes—they can help change the way they respond to the ethical challenges they face as they mature.

Why Parents Make a Difference

Taken together, these three pieces of research hint at a larger point. They suggest that when kids face compelling moral temptations, parents can make a difference. They can help their children resist moral temptations that violate their core values—our first lens, so vividly exemplified in the lie-telling experiment. Parents can also show their children how to make the kind of ethical choices that will steer them into balanced media use—our second lens. And they can encourage them to express moral courage (our third lens) in the face of whatever would challenge their authenticity and lure them into a counterfeit selfhood.

Is My Child's Moral Compass Predetermined by Nature?

But aren't our kids (some parents would counter) up against a genetic or neurobiological determinism that programs their ethics from the start? Don't these predisposing conditions trump anything a parent might do to change the ethical picture? Richard Dawkins's book *The Selfish Gene,* for instance—doesn't it tell us that our genes program us to be selfish rather than ethical? Indeed it does. But it also alerts us that we may have the capacity to overcome that programming. "Our genes may instruct us to be selfish," Dawkins writes, "but we are not necessarily compelled to obey them all our lives."[6]

Then what about peer pressure? Doesn't recent research suggest that resistance to peer influence—known as RPI, a much-studied capability that remains low in early adolescence and grows steadily between the ages of fourteen and eighteen—is all bound up in the complex activity of the brain?[7] So it is, say a group of researchers from the United Kingdom and Canada led by Marie-Heléne Grosbras. "Our results suggest that enhanced neural interactions across brain regions," they write, "underlie, at least in part, RPI in early adolescence." Yet even they don't read their findings as deterministic. Instead, they conclude that their work "may inspire the development of strategies aimed at enhancing resistance to peer pressure."

The point is that parents who are alert to the ethical challenges facing their kids can find strategies to help them survive and prosper. Consider some of the issues arising in the tween-through-teen years:

- *Cheating.* Sixty percent of twelve to seventeen year olds have friends who cheat at school, according to a 2004 ABC News Primetime poll. But do they themselves also cheat? Among twelve to fourteen year olds, 23 percent say yes—rising to 36 percent for those ages fifteen to seventeen, and peaking at 43 percent for sixteen and seventeen year olds. Among this last group, only a quarter say they've talked about cheating with their parents, compared to about 40 percent among those twelve and thirteen years old. *Message for parents:* Find ways to keep the *Don't cheat!* discussion alive into the final years of high school, since that's when children need you most.

- *Feelings about school.* Ask teens to tell you how they feel about school, and their most common adjectives are *bored* and *tired.* According to the Gallup Organization, older teens (aged sixteen and seventeen) are more likely than thirteen to fifteen year olds to "express negative feelings" about school, while younger ones are more likely to "report feeling happy, challenged, supported, and appreciated." *Message for parents:* While you might think your children are maturing toward self-sufficiency, the truth is that the

older they get, the more they may need you to deliver
the support and appreciation that's missing at school.

- *Parental monitoring.* Parents are largely clueless about
their children's online behavior. According to a 2008
Norton Online Living Report, parents think their kids
are online each month for about two hours, while kids
themselves report twenty hours. Parents also think that
only 6 percent of U.S. children have been approached
by strangers online, while 16 percent of kids say that's
happened. *Message for parents:* Get the facts, or get
some monitoring software. But mostly get into conversations about digital dangers.

But will it matter what parents do? If kids become "fully skilled
lie tellers" by, say, eight years of age, will they be impervious to
further moral development? Or will they respond positively to
ethical interventions later in life? Our research suggests the latter.
Yes, there are a lot of moral (and immoral) influences out there
bearing down on your children. But nothing in the surveys and
experiments—and certainly nothing in our own experience—
suggests that parenting is hopeless, that you might as well throw
in the towel, that kids are either saints or devils. Parents have a
crucial role to play.

Different Interventions for Different Ages

To be effective, parental interventions need to be appropriate to
the children's ages. While that sounds like a truism, it can be a
vexing issue when it comes to developing a child's moral compass.
Here, we find, our three lenses lend themselves to three developmental stages.

It makes excellent sense to address younger children—up
through age five or six—through basic character education programs that focus on our first lens: knowing what's right. That's

when kids learn to do skits about compassion, draw posters about honesty, write stories about fairness, earn prizes for responsibility, and make up songs about respect. Walk through the vendors' display booths at any national conference on character education these days, and you'll be dazzled by the colors, textures, shapes, and sounds of the materials available to help little children learn about the virtues, appreciate one another, and reject bullying. The message that comes through from the adults is simple and direct: "Kids, these are your values—always obey them all!"

That idea—always obey your values!—is a vital message that potential lie tellers need to hear at an early age. But as they mature into middle school and life grows more complicated, choices become tougher. It is here, parenting expert Michele Borba explains, that decision making becomes crucial. "In my work in schools," she writes, "I see too many children rushing to make decisions only to regret their choices later. We need to help our children learn to slow down and think through all the possible consequences that might result from their choices. Once your child has looked at all the possibilities, he is ready to begin the process of elimination. This process is immensely valuable, because it helps him think through what the outcomes might be if he puts his plan into place. It prevents him from making rash decisions that could haunt him the rest of his life."[8]

In the early years, those decisions all seem to be between obeying and disobeying a core value. They seem, in other words, to be right-versus-wrong choices. As kids mature, however, the decisions increasingly become matters of right versus right.

What seemed so simple in a right-versus-wrong world— obedience to the core values—becomes harder when both sides are right and values must be prioritized. Yet the same educational vendors so rich in products for small children have little on offer for older youth. But what are our kids to think when, for example, they find that their respect for and responsibility to others come squarely up against the requirement to tell the truth and be honest?

What do they do when a friend has sworn them to secrecy about something that could endanger the whole school—a gun in a locker, say—and the principal asks them point-blank, "What did your friend tell you?"

To an adult, such a question raises no dilemmas: of course the right thing for the child to do is to blurt out all he knows at once, since lives may be in danger. But pause for a moment and look at it through the child's eyes. He knows that truth telling is right, and he probably knows how serious this is. But he also knows that loyalty and promise keeping are also right. What's more, his entire peer culture has enforced that lesson through a devastatingly sharp vocabulary that includes words like *snitch* and *ratting*. If all the principal has to offer is ethics as a big club—"Tell me the truth, because that's the right thing to do!"—the child may well be paralyzed by the twin tensions of loyalty and truth telling. In that situation, the principal who knows about right-versus-right dilemmas will immediately find a way to begin the conversation by examining why loyalty is right and why truth is also right. Then, gently and helpfully, the principal can help the child see that if there's a choice between them, one has to trump the other in this situation. That doesn't make the other one wrong; it simply means that one of them is simply the higher right.

But suppose the principal doesn't do that and instead insists that it's simply a matter of "obeying your values." If nothing has prepared the child to understand right-versus-right dilemmas, even the most ethically minded may be forced to conclude that they can't do what their elementary school teachers said and obey all their values at once. And that discovery will bring them to a significant fork in the road. If we're fortunate, they'll find the moral and intellectual strength within themselves to develop a right-versus-right decision-making model of their own—or else they'll turn to adults who can provide that model for them. Otherwise they may well turn away from values as something they've outgrown. If our frameworks for ethical thinking give them no way to resolve complex gun-in-the-locker dilemmas where two values come into conflict, can we blame them for abandoning the whole ethics enterprise? After all, if by my middle school years I've concluded that "always obeying all values" is possible only for little kids, maybe the fact that I'm outgrowing my values is proof that I'm growing up. Maybe breaking away from my values, in the name of freedom or independence, is what real moral courage is about. Maybe, to be grown up, I've got to put up a show of bravado by defying, boldly and pugnaciously, whatever my teachers saw as ethics and integrity. Maybe I build real character by real defiance of these three lenses.

It's impossible to overstate the damage that arises from that sad but sincere philosophical conclusion. As core values and ethical reasoning get left behind, moral courage morphs into a counterfeit sort of bravado. As genuine moral courage gets left behind, ethical challenges show up at increasingly early ages:

- When fifteen-year-old Jonathan Lebed began using fictitious names to promote stocks on Yahoo Finance message boards from his New Jersey bedroom in 1999, netting some $800,000 in six months, he triggered chaos in the markets until the Securities and Exchange Commission finally nailed him for stock market fraud.

- When thirteen-year-old Megan Meier hung herself in her closet in Missouri in 2006 after a boy she'd known only on MySpace messaged her that "the world would be a better place without you"—a boy who never existed, invented as a vengeful hoax by the forty-seven-year-old mother of one of Megan's estranged girlfriends—the case sent shock waves through the world's media.

- The "I Love You" computer virus that appeared in 2000—allegedly developed and launched in the

Philippines by a lone computer student, Onel A. de Guzman—created an estimated $5.5 billion in global damages.

Each of these examples involved youth, and each puzzled legal authorities, who struggled to find laws applicable to these new technological fault lines. Yet I suspect none of these young people would have been stopped merely by having a parent say, "That's wrong! Just obey your values, and don't do it." What's needed is a comprehensive approach to the ethics of parenting that builds outward into seasoned, thoughtful structures of right-versus-right decision making and moral courage—while still resting on the foundations of shared values.

Why the Time Is Ripe for Ethical Parenting

Such an undertaking, far from being a futile task, may be beautifully timed to mesh with the conditions of our age. There may be no more promising a time for parents to muster moral courage—the third lens—and seize the initiative:

- Some 80 percent of teens now say they have "no problem" getting along with their parents—up from only 48 percent in 1974, says the National Association of Secondary School Principals.

- By a two-to-one margin, the same study shows that teens think values and character will matter more to them than to today's adults.

- Asked whether they see themselves as the "Us generation," more "oriented toward community well-being than toward ourselves," two-thirds agree.

- By large numbers, teens report that while they have strict rules at home, the rules are fair, report Neil Howe and Bill Strauss in their book *Millennials Rising*.[9]

To be sure, we may never create a generation of kids who invariably side with integrity. But we can make enormous strides in helping them hone their values-based skills as honest reporters, respectful narrators, responsible citizens, fair-minded observers, and compassionate actors.

But do I know enough, some parents ask, to address these kinds of questions with my kids? After all, as parents tell us and the research confirms, the choices are tougher today than when we were growing up. *Enron, Columbine, 9/11,* and *Iraq* weren't part of our vocabulary. Nor were *AIDS, meth,* and *date rape*—or *spam, phishing,* and *sexting.* The media weren't around 24/7, and so virulent and in your face. Workaholic adults, latchkey kids, and one-minute parenting weren't so commonplace. Besides, parents say, the social institutions that were helpful in those days—schools, political bodies, businesses, and houses of worship—can no longer cope.

Those are fair points. Although these institutions are increasingly interested in ethics, look what's happened to what were once considered to be the sources of moral guidance in our culture:

- K–12 education is overwhelmed trying to accomplish its basic three R's task.

- Governments can't legislate morality and shouldn't be asked to try.

- Corporations are torn by competitive forces and short-term imperatives.

- Faith-based groups, battling a secularizing and materialistic culture, haven't had much success inculcating morality without appearing moralistic.

That leaves one institution—the family, and particularly the parents—that can be galvanized for this purpose.

Yet many parents cringe at the thought of discussing ethics with their kids. They feel inadequate getting into conversations about truth, character, and rightness. Partly it's that they don't have the language. And partly it's that when they were young, they themselves kicked against the standards their parents and teachers set. A lot of today's parents did indeed push the envelope when they were young. They watched friends experiment with drugs, sex, and edgy behavior, and sometimes they did too. "So what gives us the right to talk about ethics?" they ask. "Won't that make us hypocrites?"

No. With maturity comes wisdom, a commitment to helping the young, and a desire to do things better than you once did. That's especially true in ethics, which gradually replaces selfishness in the arc of parental development. If your motive is to build a more ethical future for your children—and if it weren't, you wouldn't have read this far in the book—you can succeed. You'll need some easily grasped talking points, helpful guidelines, practical frameworks, and clear entryways into ethical conversations. You'll need, in other words, what the world tends to dismiss as an oxymoron: philosophy that works. That's what this book is about, as the stories in the following chapters demonstrate.

What Makes Parenting Tough?

Is parenting really harder than ever? Yes and no. A majority of adults responding to a 2007 survey by the Pew Research Center believe that parents aren't measuring up to the standards of their own parents a generation ago. It may be, however, that every generation feels that way. A Pew poll from 1997 reached nearly identical conclusions. While every age looks back at earlier ages through a golden haze, it's true that some of the challenges topping today's lists wouldn't even have been on our grandparents' minds. Consider these:

(*continued*)

Biggest Challenges in Raising Children Today	%
• **Societal factors (net)**	38
○ Society/outside influences	13
○ Drugs and alcohol	10
○ Peer pressure	7
○ TV/Internet/movies, etc.	5
○ Keeping kids from trouble	4
○ Crime/gangs/keeping kids safe	4
• **Morals/discipline/parenting (net)**	31
○ Teaching morals/right & wrong	8
○ Discipline/maintaining discipline	8
○ Being there/taking care	7
○ Teaching respect/manners	3
○ Communication w/children	2
• **Time/work balance (net)**	10
○ Time w/kids/quality time	5
○ Balance work & home	2
○ Both parents working	2
• **Costs/affording kids/finances**	8
• **Education/keeping kids in school**	7
• **Other/everything**	12
• **Don't know**	7

What makes parenting tough? Asked to define the major challenges, parents listed "teaching morals/right & wrong" as among the top challenges, outranked only by "society/outside influences" and "drugs and alcohol," and tied with "Discipline/ maintaining discipline" and "Costs/affording kids/finances."

Parents' concerns fall roughly into thirds. One set of concerns features influences from the surrounding culture— what Pew researchers call "societal factors." Another set centers on quantitative issues—the opportunity-and-money questions captured under the headings of Time, Costs, and

Education. The third set involves the qualitative issues that parents themselves face under the "Morals/discipline/parenting" heading. If the first set has its roots in sociology and the second in economics, this third set is rooted solidly in the humanities. It exists at the intersection where moral philosophy meets the skills of communication. When families have frameworks for thinking about this ethics-communication intersection—and for conversing about and discussing ethics with their kids—their children learn to negotiate these challenges with increasing confidence. Without a constructive way to think, parents are left wringing their hands helplessly over the world's ills—or desperately trying to wall off their children from outside influences. The result? They're more likely to condemn themselves and other parents for doing a bad job.

2

Birth Through Age Four

In history, as scholars often point out, weather matters. That's true for ethics as well, as Sandy discovered one bitterly cold morning in an unseasonable Missouri winter.

Branson and the Gold Coins

As she left the fabric store—her fourth stop on what should have been a quick trip to the mall—three-year-old Branson suddenly exclaimed, "Mommy, Mommy—the gold coins!" Holding him with one hand, pushing his infant sister, Molly, in a shopping cart with the other, she didn't pay attention. Her car was well across the parking lot, and she was not about to slow down in the piercing, eye-watering wind.

She got them both out of their snowsuits—no easy task in the back of a small car—and strapped into their seats. And only then, as she unloaded the cart, did she spot the little mesh bag of gold-foil-wrapped chocolate coins. She hadn't bought them—or, for that matter, anything else at the fabric store. But she vaguely recalled seeing a rack of them hanging beside the cash register. Branson must have tossed them into the cart as they were leaving.

At first she shrugged it off. It was a cheap gewgaw, more like a giveaway than a sale item. Besides, who would miss it? She finished her unpacking, got in the car, and started the engine. While her conscience made her uneasy, the thought of bundling up her children again, getting them out of the car, and trekking back into the store to return that trinket was overwhelming. Besides, she was running late and needed to get home to give them lunch and put them down for their naps.

Then it dawned on her that she could just leave the coins in the shopping cart. That way, at least, she wouldn't benefit from something she'd never bought. But that didn't work for her either, since the store would still be missing an item that apparently had been shoplifted.

In the end, what stopped her was the realization that her son was watching. He knew he'd put the coins in the cart. From his exclamation as they were leaving the store, he seemed to sense that they hadn't been paid for.

"I didn't want him ever to think, 'Hey, this is how we get stuff!'" she recalls thinking.

What Sandy was encountering was a fact as old as childbearing itself: that the presence of children in your life recalibrates your entire ethical compass. Suddenly there's another moral voice in your ear, another angel of conscience sitting on your shoulder. Now you've got someone else's way of looking at the world, where before you'd had only your own. Those young eyes aren't looking outward at the world and pondering its dilemmas. They're looking straight at you, watching to see how you negotiate moral puzzles. You are the subject and focus of their interest, their concern, their curiosity. At that age, what you do even in the small events teaches big lessons.

How Children Try to Figure Out Adults

A child's fascination with the way adults think is especially engaged, developmental psychologists tell us, around the ages of three and four—Branson's age. Younger children focus on the facts of the world as they experience it, and older ones begin to try to comprehend the thoughts and beliefs that others hold about that world—a task that will occupy them, with greater or lesser success, for the rest of their lives. Children, in other words, begin at that age to develop "the ability to predict another's actions/thoughts when they differ from [their] own." Reporting on this phenomenon in their recent book *Neuroscience of Cognitive Development: The Role of Experience and the Developing Brain*, researchers Charles A. Nelson, Michelle de Haan, and Kathleen M. Thomas describe a test in which young children are told, "Max has some chocolate, puts it away in a blue cupboard and leaves. Then his mother comes in and moves it to a green cupboard. Max comes back to get his chocolate."

The children are then asked, "'Where will Max look for the candy?' or 'Where does Max think the candy is?'" The correct answer, the researchers note, is, "Max will look in the blue cupboard because he believes the chocolate still to be there." In fact, however, "children younger than 3 to 4 years typically answer that Max will look in the green cupboard. The explanation is that, since these children know where the candy is, they incorrectly attribute to Max the same knowledge."[1]

Interestingly, new theories of neuroscience suggest that what allows older children to answer correctly is not simply that they have become better at representing the mental states of others. It is that "improvements in inhibitory control allow them more successfully to inhibit the tendency to focus on the salient fact (their knowledge of where the candy really is) and focus on the less salient but correct answer" concerning Max's belief of where the candy is.[2]

Taking Things Without Permission

Why this should be so is certainly a fascinating exercise in laboratory-based sleuthing, but it is of little practical use to Sandy on that cold morning. But that it is so may be directly relevant to her. Branson may be trying to determine not whether Sandy already knows about the gold coins and where they are (which he himself, of course, already knows), but whether there is some truth about the coins (like the fact that they haven't been paid for) that is more important than simply their presence. Branson may, in fact, be trying to figure out Sandy's thinking, which he is beginning to suspect may be different from his own. He may be seeking to comprehend not, "Where's the candy?" but, "Does Mommy think it's okay for the candy to be here?" So his outcry that frigid morning on the way to the car may be more than the self-absorbed concern of a three year old. It may be the budding of a mental process ready to encounter the beliefs, desires, and values held by the adults in his world. Perhaps Branson is seeking to learn something about the moral universe he is entering. That very morning, inconvenient though it is, he may be ready for a life lesson.

Sandy now faced a choice. She could persist in her plan for the day—which, from the point of view of hungry children who didn't much like putting on snowsuits, would be the kindest and least disruptive thing to do. Or she could seize the opportunity to turn this incident into a teachable moment. It was right, she knew, to get them home. But it was also right to return property rather than steal it—and to help Branson learn that lesson. Seen that way, the moral choice was clear: returning stolen property trumped keeping to a schedule no matter how annoying that choice might be.

In the end, Sandy found a way through her dilemma. Leaving the children in the car to stay warm, she ran back into the store. Since all the clerks were busy, she plunked the chocolate coins down on the counter and raced back to the car. She knew as she did it that this wasn't the perfect solution. Had a police officer seen her, she would have been blasted for leaving kids unattended in an automobile with the engine running. And what was the clerk to make of the mysterious appearance of chocolate coins on a counter that a few minutes earlier was clear? But in the circumstances, she felt it was the best available choice—not the ideal right, but the nearest right in the situation.

Branson had been watching carefully. "Where did you go, Mommy?" he asked when she returned somewhat breathless to the car.

"I had to take back the gold coins," she replied simply. "We can't do that. It's not right to take stuff we haven't paid for."

Is This a Moment for Teaching or for Action?

Sandy never had the luxury of planning to teach her son a lesson that day about honesty versus stealing, paying versus shoplifting, or "I take responsibility" versus "I'm too busy." Parenting doesn't work that way, especially with such young children. Of course you can plan. But those plans must make room for the unexpected, the incidental, the spontaneous. Like a compass in the wilderness, what brings you through is an internal guidance system—a set of clear moral values you carry with you. You don't always have a map. You can't always see where you're going, and you don't always know where you are. But when you know where true north is—when you know the fixed points in your own moral geography—you can keep moving without walking in circles, trusting that sooner or later you'll emerge into familiar territory.

That's what Sandy brought to this situation. As she left the house that morning, she hadn't said to herself, "Oh, I'd better remember to bring my values!" She didn't have to: they were already present, embedded deep within her, so when the moment came, they were there to guide her. Her own standards were too strong to let her abandon the moral high ground. Yes, it was a struggle, given the biting cold and the pressure of time. But in the end, she couldn't do otherwise.

Why not?

The answer lies in the moral frameworks that, whether we recognize them or not, tend to shape our reasoning in situations like this. In this case, the relevant framework is captured in the first of our three lenses—knowing what's right—and in the five core values that help us define *right* as whatever is honest, responsible, respectful, fair, and compassionate. At its simplest, Sandy's story is about knowing right from wrong. Seen from a three year old's perspective, it needs to be a tale about the core moral values of honesty and responsibility and how we put them into practice. The lesson here is crisp and sharp, leaving little room for discussion: you don't steal, and you take responsibility to set things right when you've done wrong.

But it's also a story about right versus right. After all, Sandy's challenge begins with an age-old conundrum: Is this a moment for teaching or for action? Those two noble human impulses are often at odds with each other. However much we long to instill lasting behavioral standards in our children, there are times when lesson learning must be secondary. Had Sandy watched Branson reach his hand toward a red-hot stove burner, she would no doubt have dropped everything, screamed, and raced across the kitchen to stop him. Later there would be time for discussion. Her first priority would be to keep him from burning himself.

This situation was different. Demanding no such radical reaction, it was more easily seen as an opportunity for teaching. Even so, it first came at Sandy as a right-versus-right situation, pitting the need to care for her children against the need to restore property to the store owner. Of the four paradigms identified for analyzing ethical dilemmas, this one centered on short term versus long term. The needs of Sandy's day—making sure her children weren't stretched beyond their limits and were properly fed and rested—argued for the short-term action of heading straight home. The needs of her children's education and maturation, in contrast, argued for slowing the momentum and inserting a life lesson that could stand her son in good stead for the rest of his days. Both choices were right, and she couldn't do both at once.

That cold morning, then, her dilemma was finely balanced. The arguments for driving away could not be lightly dismissed. If they'd been real gold coins, of course, she wouldn't have hesitated to return them. But if one of her children were suddenly ill or if her husband had called with an emergency, she wouldn't have flinched at driving away. To be sure, her children's needs for lunches and naps were no emergency, but they weren't insignificant either, especially given the thoughts that can so easily assail conscientious parents in such situations:

- Am I stretching my children too thin?

- Did I really need to make this trip to the mall, or was I just being selfish because I wanted to get out of the house?

- Am I too lax in my scheduling, leaving too late from home and wasting too much time in the first stores I visit?

- Or am I too rigid in my plans, never leaving room to deal with the time-consuming stuff that always happens when kids are young?

- Or am I just too uptight, making mountains out of molehills and seeing huge ethical issues in something some other moms might shrug off as trivial?

This line of reasoning—an elaborate set of self-engendered suggestions about guilt, blame, and self-condemnation—can sweep in so rapidly that within seconds, we've arrived at a stark conclusion: *I'm a bad parent!* In Sandy's case, notice how seductively this reasoning wants to lead her to abandon her moral intuitions. *Okay, I'm a bad mom*, it wants her to say, *so to make up for that, I'm going to put my children's immediate needs first, ignore these wretched coins, and head straight home*. Thus does guilt, by its curious logic, become self-justification, tempting us to put aside the demands of ethics in the name of parenting.

Distinguishing Mountains from Molehills: Five Tests for Wrongdoing

In the end, perhaps the most common temptation of parenting is this false dichotomy that says, "You've got to choose between parenting and ethics. You can't have it both ways. Which is it going to be?" To her credit, Sandy had the strength to resist this line of reasoning—the toughest part of which, no doubt, would have been that final bullet point about mountains and molehills. Are we sure this is no mere molehill? How often we find our children accusing us of just this sort of mountain making—railing against some moral stand we've taken by announcing petulantly, "Everybody else's parents let them do it!" and, "You're the only parents in the whole world who are so strict!" That conversation usually occurs when adolescents are beginning to experience a larger world outside the home and draw comparisons. It would be surprising, in fact, to hear three-year-old Branson make this case. But just because Sandy's children aren't yet four, don't think for a moment that she herself is untouched by these arguments. The false rationale doesn't come from her children. Instead it comes from herself as she applies that seductive phrase about making mountains out of molehills to her own life. Is this really a moral issue, or is Sandy just moralizing? Does this matter, or does she need to lighten up and let go? How can she tell what's right?

One way she can tell is by applying our the tests for wrongdoing. If the issue Sandy faced were merely a molehill, she could easily find her way past each of the following tests. In fact, as these tests make clear, the case of the gold coins actually is something of a mountain:

- *The legal test.* Shoplifting, however inadvertent, is illegal. Parents have a legal responsibility for the actions of their children in this regard. And they certainly have an obligation to avoid complicity in their children's stealing. They need to bring it to light and set it right, rather than hide it and thereby condone it.

- *The regulatory test.* The legal test, as it applies to stealing, is strong and clear. So any additional regulations (from the mall, say, or from some social or religious organization to which Sandy might belong) would serve to reinforce what the law had already said.

- *The stench test.* Sandy's gut-level response is that taking stuff without paying smells really bad. Given that intuition, she's already found that she can't ignore the issue and let the coins go unreturned.

- *The front-page test.* How would she feel if, in tomorrow morning's paper, a headline shouted, "Local Mom Nabbed at Mall in Gold-Coin Heist"? If she chose to drive away—and if her every action were fully captured on surveillance cameras, analyzed by detectives, and published by journalists—she would be deeply embarrassed and roundly shamed.

- *The Mom test.* In this situation, can she imagine her own mom—or some other exemplar whose moral standards she admires—doing what she's about to do? Under normal circumstances, such people would never deliberately drive away without returning the coins.

What's clear from this process is that the case of the coins, however small, presents only one right answer. We don't know the details of Sandy's thinking here—indeed, she herself can't recall exactly how she reasoned it out. But we do know the outcome: despite all the arguments in favor of driving away, it didn't take her long to dismiss them, return the coins, and transform this interruption into a lesson for her son.

Beyond that, there's also a lesson for Sandy herself. In the end, it's clear that she wasn't facing a right-versus-right issue after all. It may have felt that way at the outset, but ultimately she could see that this wasn't a question of two competing right courses of action. Even the briefest analysis showed that all the moral weight lay on one side. She had no need for an extended analytical conversation about tough dilemmas with herself or her son. Instead, she saw that the focus needed to be on the difference between right and wrong. Yes, it took her a few minutes to grasp that point. Sure, she could have resolved the issue more quickly had she seen it that way from the beginning. Perhaps if it hadn't been so bitterly cold, she wouldn't have been in such a hurry to cross that parking lot. Maybe if she hadn't had somewhere else to get to, she would have paid more attention to what Branson had said. It might have happened that in a more relaxed moment, she would have taken an interest in his initial alarm about gold coins rather than just chalking it up to his fanciful imagination. Looking back, she knew she should have found out what he meant. "At that moment," she said, "I should have just turned right back around and run back into the store."

But she also needs to cut herself some slack. There's nothing strange or shameful about her response. One of the toughest things we face as adults is knowing when to break the momentum of our daily chores in the face of a moral challenge. One mark of our ethical fitness, in fact, is how accurately we read such situations and how quickly we respond. It's a talent every parent must develop, lest moments of ethical significance slide right past us—a point about which we'll have more to say later in the book.

Stealing the Penny Gumball

For Ginny, it's never too early to teach kids not to steal. Nor is the thing stolen too small to be a worthwhile example, even if it's only a penny gumball.

When her son was three, he stole a piece of bubble gum from a store. Actually, she admits, "it wasn't really stealing," since it had come from a gumball machine and fallen on the floor after someone else had paid for it. But, she says, "it was the perfect example" to teach him a lesson.

They were in the car when she noticed in the rear-view mirror that he was chewing something.

"What have you got in your mouth?"

"I've got some gum, Mom."

"Where did you get that?"

"I got it from the store, on the floor."

"So you took something you didn't pay for?"

"But it was on the floor."

"But you took something you didn't pay for?"

"Yes."

"We're going to go talk to the store manager."

She took him back and made him apologize and pay the penny. Since then, she said, "I've never had a problem" with his honesty.

"I raised him never to lie about anything," she recalls. "I told him that the minute you start lying to people, you lie to yourself. And then you can't go to sleep at night, because you don't know who you've lied to and who you haven't. One lie leads to another, and before you know it, you don't even know who you are, because you've lied so much that it changes who you are. So don't ever start lying."

She also told him that "if you've done something bad, the best thing you can do is come to me and tell me before someone else does." Even now, at age eighteen, he doesn't lie to her about anything. "If he's smoking pot," she says, "he's going to tell me, even though it isn't something acceptable. He's going to tell me—he's not going to lie."

While she has encountered plenty of complex challenges with her kids along the way, Ginny says, the question of lying is straightforward. On that topic, "I really don't think there are a lot of gray areas in this life," she says. "I think a lot of it is black and white."

Branson and the Gold Coins

- *Knowing* what's right (lens 1) and *doing* what's right are different things. Don't beat yourself up if it takes a while to discover how to do what you know is right.
- Young children learn by watching your choices. Talk to them about honesty and responsibility, but remember that what matters is how you yourself practice those values.
- Like many other things in life, doing right takes work. Ethics is often inconvenient and sometimes tough. Be willing to go out of your way to teach moral lessons.
- People with strong moral compasses are sometimes subject to self-condemnation. Don't let guilt make you think you must choose between good ethics and good parenting.
- Sticking to your plan is a mark of conscientiousness. Breaking a plan to seize a teachable moment is a mark of conscience. Knowing which to do is the genius of true parenting.

Teaching Responsibility

The need for us to teach responsibility to small children, as Sandy learned, can be demanding—even, at times, annoying. In her case, the teachable moment arose from an incident brought on by her child's actions. For Eric, by contrast, that opportunity grew from a life-threatening choice he himself had to make. And while he too could have walked right past this teachable moment, he chose to share his discomforting but instructive tale with his young daughters.

A Father Chooses to Explain His Hunting Adventure

On a late October day, Eric Caylor and two friends were in northern Wisconsin bow hunting for deer. In the morning, as they staked out their territories, Eric chose a knoll well away from the others, about a quarter-mile from his parked truck. With a good view of the surrounding area, he figured he didn't need to climb the lone tree on top of the knoll. Instead, he built a blind on the ground out of logs and branches and settled down to wait for the deer to pass by.

Nothing much happened that morning. But late in the afternoon, the bears arrived—coming up behind him, out of his line of vision, and foraging so quietly that he never heard them. It wasn't until he stood up to leave the blind in the waning light that he found himself face-to-face with a cub. Eric tried to scare it off. But the cub, confused by the sudden spectacle of an arm-waving creature in camouflage, didn't run away. Instead, it ran right past him and climbed the tree.

Instinctively Eric looked around for the mother bear. She would be within fifteen to twenty feet of him, he guessed, and would have three more cubs in tow. In that brief and intense moment, he weighed his options. While he knew he was in good physical shape—he earned his living as a professional diver—he also knew he couldn't outrun a bear. Nor could he escape by climbing the tree, since her cub was already up there. If she charged, his only course would be to shoot her with his bow, head-on. As a woodsman with great love of nature and its ways, he instinctively recoiled at the thought of depriving those cubs of their mother. He also knew there were serious penalties for killing a bear without a permit. Yet he knew that he could be facing a choice between his life and hers.

In fact, he faced five tough moral choices. Within seconds, his first decision—*Do I shoot?*—demanded an answer. The bear charged. Eric shot, the arrow hitting its target. She somersaulted, landing almost at his feet. Then she scrambled up and lumbered away.

Not knowing which way she would go, Eric dashed for his truck and roared down the rough logging road, honking to warn his friends lest they too encounter a bear that was not only angry but seriously wounded. When they met up and he told them the story, they all concluded that Eric's second choice—*Do I report this incident?*—had only one answer: yes. Hushing it up to keep him out of trouble with the law was tempting. But to keep it quiet would not only endanger the cubs, whose survival could be in question; it could also endanger other hunters or home owners in the area. Eric had escaped without a mauling. What if others weren't so fortunate?

From hunting in this area before, Eric was aware that the local Department of Natural Resources warden was known for being, as he said, "a stickler." Even so, as soon as they reached the highway and got into cell phone range, Eric called him. From his first words, the warden appeared to be living up to his reputation. With an eight-year wait for the few Wisconsin licenses given out each year to hunt bears—and with no attacks on humans by bears ever recorded in the history of the county—the warden wasn't about to buy Eric's self-defense story. He told Eric to meet him at the site early the next morning. He wanted to check out the knoll.

That evening, Eric called his wife to let her know what had happened. His two daughters, aged nine and four, were already in bed. So his answer to his third decision—*Do I tell the kids?*—was made easier: *Not yet.* He asked his wife to say nothing about the incident. Given his daughters' love for animals and the anguish this tale could cause, he knew that if the story were to be told— and perhaps it needn't be—he would have to be the teller. Why, they would ask, had Daddy killed a bear and left her cubs without a mother?

In the morning, Eric and his friends drove back to the logging road, accompanied now by his brother and his ten-year-old nephew, who had arrived overnight. As the four waited at the truck, Eric walked with the warden and his assistant to the knoll. Everything at the site—the blind, the scuff marks on the ground, the blood on the leaves, the cub's claw marks on the tree, the snapped branches where the mother bear had fled—supported Eric's story. After studying the situation, the wardens told him he was free to go without paying a fine. But they left him to decide whether to try to track down the bear. If he found her alive, they told him, he would have to put her down, any way he could, since she almost certainly could not survive the coming winter in her wounded state. He would then have to call them to come and get the body. He wouldn't be allowed to keep the meat, due to a policy intended to keep unethical hunters from killing game and then claiming it was an accident. Instead, the wardens would be sure the meat went to Paul's Pantry, a local community food bank, or to some other charitable organization.

That faced Eric with his fourth decision: *Do I give up my last chance to get a deer this season?* This was the final day of their only hunting trip of the year. None of them had yet bagged the deer their permits allowed them to take. But they all agreed that their obligation was to find the bear. The odds were significantly against them. Not only was it tough to track her through the swampy area around the knoll, but a heavy overnight rain had further obscured whatever telltale signs she had left. Nevertheless, nearly ten hours and a few lucky breaks later, they came upon her—with her cubs. It fell to Eric to finish her off, which he did with a single, heart-wrenching bow shot. Her cubs fled.

After field-dressing the carcass and lugging it back to their truck, Eric contacted the warden. He met them several hours later at Eric's cabin. When he saw the bear, he complimented Eric for being honest from the start and calling him right away. He noted, too, that although Eric and his group could have just walked away from the situation and spent the weekend hunting as usual, they had instead gone beyond the call of duty to track down a wounded animal. It seemed only fair, he said, that Eric be rewarded in some way. So he offered Eric the bear for the cost of the twenty-five-dollar permit, which Eric accepted.

Now, however, came the fifth decision: *How do I tell the kids I've killed a bear?* Eric felt strongly about the need for truth telling with his children. Even if he hadn't, however, saying nothing was no longer an option. In his family's hunting culture, it would be impossible to pass off bear meat as venison. Even at their age, his children knew that while everyone hunted deer, hardly anyone got to hunt bear.

So when Eric called home, he asked to speak to his daughters. Nine-year-old Lorelei was, as he had guessed, deeply upset about the cubs. Eric told her that he too had been worried. So he had talked to some old-timers in the area and told them how big the cubs were. They had assured him the cubs were old enough to take care of themselves and would be fine. That comforted her somewhat.

Then four-year-old Anneleise got on the phone. As he was explaining what happened, she stopped him.

"But Daddy," she said, "you don't have a *license* to shoot bears!"

Eric told her she was right, but said he hadn't had a choice.

"Are you going to try to get away with it?" she asked.

"No," said Eric. "I told the truth. Even though I thought I might get in trouble, I still told the truth. And I *didn't* get in trouble, *because* I told the truth."

How Eric's Five Choices Reflect Core Values

Eric's story is not the happiest of tales—especially if you don't share his views on hunting. But within the standards of that sport—especially as practiced in rural American communities where a freezer full of venison can recalibrate the entire family budget—the values Eric expressed are strongly embedded. His first decision—*Do I shoot?*—was perhaps more reflexive than rational, more self-protective than ethical. But even that decision grew out of his intuitions. Honed by years of experience, shaped by a confidence in his skill with a bow and arrow, they allowed him to stand firm where others might have panicked. And while he probably wouldn't have said it this way in those few fleeting moments, he was up against a values-driven choice. On one hand, he faced the prospect of a mother bear leaving behind her cubs. On the other, he faced the possibility of leaving behind a widow and two children. As his daughter Lorelei knew, there was a powerful case to be made that Eric had a responsibility for the mother bear's life. Even more powerfully, however, he knew she could see the case for his responsibility to his family, his community, and himself.

Responsibility, in fact, is one of five core, shared values that appears to be innate in the human condition. At the Institute for Global Ethics, we've spent several decades asking people around the world to define the ethical values that matter most to them. We've asked them to identify the handful of moral virtues they would most like to see on a code of ethics, or embodied in their children, or underpinning every human interaction within their culture. In their answers, responsibility almost always surfaces among the top five. It goes by a variety of names: accountability, duty, obedience, loyalty, and other words or phrases. At heart, however, these words all describe a moral quality so basic, so universal, and so unavoidable that it surfaces strongly in every country in which we've asked these questions.

Responsibility is not the only value to surface in this way. As we do this work through surveys, interviews, focus groups, and workshop exercises, we find four other values rounding out a kind of five-starred constellation that defines a global code of ethics: honesty, respect, compassion, and fairness.[3]

Ask people to define their top five values, in other words, and they identify these ideas with uncanny commonality—often to the point of using these identical words. Ask them to define a second set of five—numbers six through ten—and the answers vary widely

Figure 2.1 Global Code of Ethics

from cohort to cohort or country to country. Limit people to five, however, and the pattern is remarkably consistent.

Why that should be so is a question worthy of serious academic speculation. Are we hardwired with a genetic set of five values? Do they inhere as neuroscientific impulses within the brain? Are core values a protection device to ensure the survival of the community? Are they spiritually derived from a divine, deific source? Have they evolved over time? Did they develop as a means for preserving the authority of the elder generation? Are they the ultimate essentials of happiness? These are all valid questions.

From a parent's perspective, however, it's less important to analyze this research than to apply it. The fact that this set of values is so universal helps answer a question deeply troubling to our culture: What is ethics? Left unanswered, it's a question that tricks many parents into believing that they can't even begin to talk about values with their children, that they don't know enough, and that they have no right to speak about things they can't define. But based on these values, the answer is plain: ethics is about being honest, responsible, respectful, fair, and compassionate. In other words, when we find ourselves in the presence of any one of the values, we naturally say, "That's good," or "That's right," or, "That's ethical."

This research is important for two reasons. First, it gives solid ammunition for countering the "Ethics? Schmethics!" response—the cynical assertion that *ethics* is nothing but a fuzzy and incomprehensible word for a fanciful and subjective notion. In fact, these five terms provide a remarkably precise definition. That's a particularly useful point in parenting, where at times *ethics* becomes simply "the e-word" that confuses people or puts them off. Parents who see that response coming can swap their vocabulary, leaving behind "ethics" and talking instead about responsibility, or respect, or fairness, or honesty, or compassion.

Second, these shared values help disable another sneering question: "Whose values will you teach?" This question isn't searching for an answer so much as demanding a capitulation. It's meant to imply that ethics is merely personal and subjective, so everyone is entitled to his or her own set of values. The argument is usually slammed down as a trump card to squelch any attempt to teach ethics—since, by this standard, ethics teaching (*character education*, as it's known in the United States, or *values education* in the United Kingdom) is nothing but an insidious attempt to impose your values on my consciousness. If, however, there are five core global values, the answer to, "Whose values?" goes something like this: "How about the universal values held by every culture, race, ethnicity, gender, political stripe, economic community, and age cohort across time?" Parents will find this idea helpful in addressing the argument that ethics is simply an effort to enforce conformity, limit creativity, and strip children of their individual characters and identities. While it's true that individuality resides in a multitude of things that differentiate us one from another, ethics unites us. Like having eyes or being able to tell sweet things from sour, our set of values is not a point of difference but of commonality.

Applying the Other Values: Honesty, Respect, Fairness, Compassion

If responsibility seemed prominent as Eric answered his first question, how did the other four values play out? Go back to his second question—*Do I report the incident?* Behind this question are issues of honesty—or candor, truthfulness, transparency, or openness. For Eric, honesty was not up for negotiation. Not to report would have been to engage in a deliberate deception, a duplicitous cover-up of a glaring fact. Remember that it was on this topic of truth telling that his four year old questioned him most insistently—and that it was his willingness to speak truthfully that allowed him to turn his experience into a crucial lesson for her: "I *didn't* get in trouble *because* I told the truth."

Like Branson with his gold coins, Anneleise was busy observing, contemplating, and analyzing her parent's every move. The world is full of such children who get their values early. Who knows where they get them—but who doubts that they have them? Recent studies suggest that even eight month olds have a sense of justice that leads them to applaud puppets acting as good guys— and to punish bad guys. "Humans do have a rudimentary moral sense from the very start of life," writes Yale psychologist Paul Bloom. "Babies possess certain moral foundations—the capacity and willingness to judge the actions of others, some sense of justice, gut responses to altruism and nastiness."[4] If you doubt that, try dividing a piece of pie unevenly between preschoolers and seeing how quickly one of them cries out, "That's not *fair!*"

Faced with temptations, of course, small children can become skilled lie tellers—as Victoria Talwar's research on lying behavior has suggested. But deep inside, it seems, they also carry a moral compass that they long to put into practice. At that age, they can watch parents shuffle, withhold, and equivocate—or they can watch them stand firm and speak straight. It is at these moments that the compass—a baby's "naive morality," as researchers call it—gets calibrated.

The third question in Eric's story—*Do I tell the kids?*—centers on a third value: respect. Sensitive to his children's concerns, he wanted them to benefit from his own understanding and explanation. By the answer he chose—*I'll tell them later*—he was waiting until he could help them grasp the significance of the situation and recognize that he too felt the conflict. But what if his answer had been, *No, I'll never tell!* Would that have been honest? Probably not. The point for parents is that waiting for the right time to express a tactful and tender respect for others can be absolutely right. But the waiting, if extended too long, can lapse into low-grade deception. In courts of law, judges sometimes postpone trials to give each side time to assemble its case. But even as they do so, they recognize the harrowing truth behind the old adage that "justice delayed is justice denied." Postponement out of concern for others' sensitivities is a highly ethical action. Postponement that extends itself into a denial of others' rights is an insidious immorality.

One of the drivers behind Eric's fourth question—*Do I give up my last chance to get a deer this season?*—is the value of fairness, variously defined as justice, equity, or equality. In this situation, applying fairness could be problematic. Plenty of people are willing to assert their right to be fairly treated—even if that right imposes unfair obligations on others. Because he didn't want to be unfair to his friends, he had ample justification for thinking, "Look, I did my bit yesterday about this bear, and I'm not going to let the entire season slip out of my hands just because of some little incident. Besides, my friends are counting on my being part of the group—and they deserve to get their deer. If I played the martyr and asked them to hunt their deer while I go track my bear, they'd be too ashamed to let me go alone. That could wreck their hunting trip. So the fairest thing to them is not to go after the bear."

But fairness also urges Eric to pursue the bear. Hunters today are familiar with the late-nineteenth-century concept of "fair chase." As defined by the Boone and Crockett Club, an organization for

North American big game hunters that dates from 1887, fair chase is "the ethical, sportsmanlike, and lawful pursuit and taking of any free-ranging wild, native North American big game animal in a manner that does not give the hunter an improper advantage over such animals."[5] By 1925 Saxton Pope, known as the father of modern bow hunting, was seeing this "improper advantage" as a denial of fairness. "It is not the killing that brings satisfaction, it is the contest of skill and cunning," he wrote. "The true hunter counts his achievement in proportion to the effort involved and the fairness of the sport."[6] Fairness is also seen to extend to a hunter's relationship to wounded animals. "Search for an arrow hit or bullet hit animal that is wounded for as long as possible," says "A Hunter's Rule" posted on the Huntingnet.com Web site, adding that hunters should "always assist a fellow hunter who needs help tracking a hit or wounded animal."[7]

Eric's decision to track the bear, then, grows up out of his sense of fairness—particularly the expectations of fairness specific to his sport. In this case, fairness required him to search for wounded animals—an interpretation of this value that would be foreign, even astonishing, in most other contexts. Real estate agents, for instance, would have no more need for an ethical code requiring them to track wounded animals than hunters would have for a code prohibiting racial discrimination in purchasing or selling property. Yet fairness underlies both. The point is that values often take on special meanings in different contexts—a useful idea for parents who, as they help their children unpack a value like fairness, can encourage them to see its very different applications in, say, the chess club, the 4-H program, the swim team, or the student elections. They can also see its wide application in challenges as different as bike riding on a neighbor's property, downloading music from the Web, or cutting into line at the movie theater.

The predominant value in Eric's fifth decision—*How do I tell the kids?*—is compassion. Given his children's love for animals, he knew he needed to honor their feelings. That required time and attention, which, even if expressed over the phone rather than in face-to-face conversation, could still be characterized by such words as *warm*, *affectionate*, *caring*, *kind*, *empathetic*, or *loving*. Suspecting his children would each focus on different concerns, he knew the situation called for one-on-one conversations—neither a foursome with both parents talking to the children together, nor a threesome with both children on the line together with their father. That way, he was able to talk to his older daughter about the issue that most concerned her—the fate of the cubs—and then defend his own honesty with her younger sister. Looking back on it, Eric also realized that there was a third child involved: his ten-year-old nephew who helped in the search. The lesson he took away, says Eric, is that "when things get tough, don't give up. Keep going. Keep trying. If this doesn't work, try something else."

If there's one value that for Eric seems to stand out in this experience, it is responsibility. For him, one of society's most serious problems is that people refuse to take responsibility for their actions. "If you're going to get into trouble," he reminds his children, "you take responsibility for your own actions."

Lessons from **Teaching Responsibility**

- Core values drive our decisions in moments of crisis as well as in times of reflection. In Eric's story, self-defense trumped law-abiding action though each embodied responsibility.
- A single incident often illustrates multiple values—not surprising, given that "knowing what's right" means understanding ethics as a reflection of all five values.
- In a world where lying can seem useful, children need to see truth telling rewarded. Had Eric lied, he would

(*continued*)

have brought home neither a deer nor a bear—only
a big fine.

- Telling everything *now* is different from telling everything
  right. Your obligation to say something doesn't deprive you
  of your right to choose how and when to say it.

Playing According to Your Own Rules

For Eric, ethics happened quietly, in one-on-one conversations
with his children. It can also happen in an auditorium full of
parents.

On a warm spring evening, the parents had come from independent schools around the Bay Area in California, eager to find
ways to help their children navigate the increasingly complex
world of moral decision making. As the speaker, I wasn't there to
give them advice about specific situations. My task was to help
them understand how to think, not what to think. I'd told them
that much from the outset. I'd then shared a number of stories,
laid out some broad ethical frameworks, and given them an inven-
tory of concepts and entry points for talking about ethics with their
children. For the question period, I'd invited not only their comments but their own stories.

As we approached the end of the evening, the air was full of
tales of ethical dilemmas and moral temptations. That's when a
young mother somewhat hesitantly raised her hand.

"I know you said you weren't going to give us advice," she said.
"But if I tell you something that happened to me, can you tell me
whether I did the right thing?"

I told her we'd all try to help. So she explained that she had
recently accompanied her husband on a business trip to a resort
hotel with their four-year-old son. One day she was lounging
beside the hot tub with her son, who was sitting quietly on the
edge, partway into the water. It was a sunny midweek afternoon,

with no one else around, and they were both enjoying the moment—until a hotel attendant came by.

"How old are you?" he asked the boy.

"Four."

The attendant apologized, pointed to a sign saying that children under five were not permitted in the hot tub, and said he would have to get out entirely.

The boy shot his mom a crushed look. Beckoning him to her side, she thanked the attendant, who left. Then she told her son that she knew how much he loved the water, and that since there was nobody else around, she thought it would be okay if he went back and sat with his legs in the water.

He started for the hot tub and then looked back for a moment.

"If the man comes back," he asked her, "what should I say?"

"Tell him you're five," she said.

There was an audible gasp from our audience in the gym.

"I know, I know," she burst out in chagrin. "My husband couldn't believe I said that!" But she explained that her son was having such a good time and wasn't bothering anybody—and that it just didn't seem like a big deal.

Given the hour we'd just spent together on ethics, it was clear to us all that she'd sent her son a troubling message about truth telling. I didn't have to tell her what I thought: the whole audience came down thumpingly on her husband's side. But she wasn't defensive. She had shared her story with disarming candor, genuinely puzzled at what had happened to her during the few seconds it took her to respond to her son's question.

Building Ethical Fitness

What followed was a wide-ranging conversation about how much your principles are worth. Would you sacrifice them for twenty minutes of enjoyment at a hot tub? Or for five dollars when you buy an under-eight ticket for your nine year old at a fair? Or for a hundred-dollar tax refund from a dubious deduction? Or for a million-dollar bonus based on falsified corporate accounts? Or for a muddled sense of ethics planted early in your four-year-old son?

Put that way, most of us would holler, "Never!" And we would mean it—at least in principle, without the pressure of a real-life temptation breathing down our necks and with ample time to think. Which is exactly what that young mother didn't have. The situation came upon her without a shred of warning. Cutting at right angles across her sense of peace, beauty, and restfulness, the sudden and unforeseen appearance of that attendant seemed to threaten one of those all-too-rare moments in a parent's life, when what you most want to do squares exactly with what makes your child happy. The question from her son, posed in midstep, called out for an immediate and caring response. It was an occasion where what mattered was not whether she was able to figure out what was right, but whether she'd already done that calculation and found the answer. There was no time to think—or so it seemed. It was, in other words, a perfect test of her ethical fitness—her trained and practiced ability to respond to ethical challenges with sure-footed immediacy and unlabored grace.

Ethical fitness is not unlike physical fitness. You're not born into it. Nor do you get it all at once by running twenty miles in a single day. Becoming physically fit isn't an inoculation. Nor is it like buying a hammer that will be in your toolbox forever, or permanently adding Maine to the list of states you've finally visited. It's a process. You get it by putting in a little effort each day, gradually toning up the muscles and extending the endurance. When the moment comes to use it, you're ready. That hundred-yard sprint through the terminal as the airplane door is closing, that dive into the lake to save the struggling puppy, that sudden need to carry Grandma from the car to the porch in the pouring rain: when you're fit, these come easily. In such cases, you don't say to yourself, "I'm not really in shape for this. I think I'll go to the Y every morning for the next three weeks and work out hard, and *then* I'll come back and catch the flight, save the pup, and help

Granny!" Fitness doesn't work that way. The readiness it demands requires constant attention lest the fitness slip away into a shadow of itself. Fitness once attained is no guarantee of fitness forever.

That's just as true in ethics as in physiology. As I've argued in my book *How Good People Make Tough Choices*, there's no guarantee that your past, by itself, will equip you with ethical fitness.

> You may come from the most moral, high-minded, right-thinking family in the world—and that's a help. You may have been well schooled and well churched, raised in a community of honest and hard-working folks—and that makes it much easier to be ethical yourself. You may have taken ethics courses in school, or worked for someone who was a model of uprightness, or gone through ethics training courses on the job—all to the good. You may even have the good fortune to live with a highly moral spouse and work in an environment where your colleagues and superiors are naturally inclined toward honesty, fairness, and a deep respect for one another—which is terrific. But that doesn't necessarily mean you're ethically fit.[8]

What's needed, in addition, is an ongoing commitment to think hard about ethical issues, grapple with tough dilemmas, and engage mentally with the various arguments for right and wrong. What's more, you've got to care about these issues and engage in a life of feeling as well as thinking. You can work out in a Pilates program without giving a fig for others in the gym—and while your thoughts are further away than Jupiter. But building ethical fitness requires mental attention. To be sure, ethics is highly rational, which is why it can readily be discussed by parents and children. But it's also rooted in intuition. Founded on the bedrock of our core moral values, which are themselves intuitional, it appears to operate through a sense of rightness that we apprehend almost

without conscious thought. "I can't put my finger on it," we sometimes say, "but this just seems wrong!"—reflecting our recognition
that an intuition has been triggered before we've applied any
reasoning to it. The process that follows—of finding a logical basis
for those feelings—is akin to the one that a literary critic or a
musicologist uses to explain why this turn of phrase or those bars
of music strike us as beautiful, ominous, sad, or uplifting. Just as a
practiced art lover can instantly "read" a painting for its impact
and put into words the reason it calls up a particular emotion, so
an ethically fit parent learns to sense the presence or absence of
values-based thought and moral behavior and to address it in
helpful ways with his or her children. That fitness can be learned,
developed, and shared. But if it is then left unpracticed, it can
atrophy, wither, and vanish.

Applying Right-Versus-Right Decision Making

Sitting by the hot tub that day, our California mother was at the
starting gate for ethical fitness. She needed it. All she lacked was
the practice. Over time, with the help of her husband, she came
to see how she could have done better. And judging from the
tone of her narrative in the gym that night, she probably felt
an intuition of wrongdoing even while she was talking to her
son. But so powerful were the atmospherics of the moment—
the warm sun, the rare relaxation, the harmony of the mother-
and-child moment—that they probably overrode that intuition.
Reasoning, too, played a role. As she told us, it didn't seem like a
big deal to break the hotel's rule, which struck her as having no
real application to her situation. The sign by the pool must have
looked to her, in that moment, like something management posted
for its own convenience. Perhaps it was meant to prevent unruly
children from annoying other adults in the crowded confines of a
hot tub. Or maybe it was designed to comply with a liability insur-
ance policy, requiring posted warnings lest irresponsible mothers
let their children get hurt playing in the tub. How easy, then, for

this mother to say, with nanosecond rationality, "There's nobody else in sight, and I'm right here keeping a watchful eye on my boy!" And what a small step it may have appeared, linguistically, to give her son an easy way out—"Tell him you're five"—in case another attendant appeared.

If, in that moment, the issue had risen to the level of a right-versus-right discussion, she could have seen it as a choice of honesty (to the regulation) versus loyalty (to her son). In that context, she could have found scores of arguments for loyalty, rooted in such core values as compassion for her son's joyful and innocent play, respect for his quiet obedience, and fairness in the face of a regulation that seemed grossly unfair.

But look for a moment at the arguments for honesty—the side of the paradigm to which her husband, and our entire audience, instantly gravitated. To them, the issue was not about a boy's relation to a hot tub. It was about a mother's relation to the truth. Her willingness to create a specialized, purpose-built lie as a way to counter a possible challenge from another attendant tells us something about her lack of acquaintance with her own core values. She didn't have a history of deception or a pathological duplicity—or so we can assume from her willingness to share publicly a story guaranteed to raise howls of moral protest from the audience. Yet she was willing not only to invent the lie but to coach her own son to tell it. In the hierarchy of teachable moments, this one goes a step beyond Sandy's experience with Branson and the gold coins. He risked no more than being an observer of a mother's wrongdoing. Here at the hot tub, by contrast, this lad was being actively inducted into the byways of deceit. No wonder her husband saw this as a mountain rather than a molehill.

Here again, then, is a case where the application of a right-versus-right framework allows us to uncover a right-versus-wrong temptation. If the question is (as we now see it), "Should I deprive my son of a few minutes of enjoyment or actively teach him to lie?" the choice is a no-brainer—at least for those who care about ethics.

What does this say about ethical fitness? For starters, this mother won't do *that* again! As this story unfolded in her life, she began moving up the scale of moral awareness. First, even at the outset, her choice seems to have bothered her: Why else would she tell her husband something he never would have otherwise known? Second, her husband made his feelings known immediately and convincingly. Third, an entire audience agreed with him. Given all that, I think we can safely say she learned a lesson.

But will she, in other situations, equivocate with rules she doesn't understand? Perhaps she will, unless she comes to understand that rule following, in the absence of clear urgencies to the contrary, is a good thing: of course you put aside the rules and trespass on your absent neighbor's property to check out the smoke coming from her basement. The problem comes when, under unexceptional conditions, we encounter rules whose rationales we don't fully understand. This mother wouldn't dream of letting her son disobey a sign that said, "No playing near the cliffs"—especially if the overhanging ground was already crumbling away and the drop-off was a thousand feet. But without a similarly compelling logic, what's the justification for not playing in the hot tub?

The answer came in a note from a member of our institute, Trip Barthel, who wrote from Shanghai shortly after I shared this mother's story in my weekly column. Noting that "there is a very practical reason for the restriction" on under-fives in hot tubs, he explained that "the younger the child, the greater the ability to absorb heat or cold, related to the surface-to-weight ratio. In other words, a young child will absorb heat much more rapidly, putting him at risk far quicker than an adult."

"Telling the truth," he concluded, may be one thing for "age requirements at a movie theater, but it has very different consequences with a hot tub."

And that raises a crucial point about rules. For the ethically fit parent, obedience to rules becomes the increasingly natural default position. Even if the rule is odd or inexplicable, the first and immediate response should be one of agreement rather than resistance. That's morally obvious if, as in this case, the teachable moment is so potent. But that position also illustrates another vital point for parenting, which is that you don't know what you don't know. This mother didn't know there was a significant physiological reason for obedience. Knowing it, she would never have put herself in that position in the first place. That's not grounds for condemnation. None of us knows half of what we should know. What's more, we have no idea of the importance of the things we don't know. Given that fact, the only safe thing to do—as adults, but especially as parents—is to give the rule the benefit of the doubt and help our children learn to do the same.

Lessons from   **Playing According to Your Own Rules**

- Asking, "What are your principles worth?" helps separate core values from mere desires. Start with small examples, ramping up to greater consequences to make the point.
- Ethical fitness prepares you to address dilemmas confidently, however suddenly they arise. The more you work through tough choices, the more easily you stay in shape.
- Developing moral intuitions about the core values—learning to listen when things don't feel ethically right—is an essential first step on which to build rational discussion.
- Sharing ethical quandaries with others is hugely helpful. Had this mom not told her husband, her son might never have benefited from his mom's greater clarity in the future.

Loren Wrecks the Train

Having a four year old who sits peacefully by a hot tub may strike some parents as a phenomenal luxury. More commonplace, perhaps, is the child who never sits still—the kid with more gusto and drive than the Energizer bunny.

As a two year old, Loren was just such a character. After a jam-packed day, he still needed to scamper around the block with his parents to burn off extra energy before bedtime. During the day, his mother, Gray, found that the best way to give herself a short break from his high-intensity living was to let him watch TV. With Loren focused on something besides his mom for half an hour, she could at last catch her breath and perhaps accomplish one small task. "How do you get anything done otherwise?" she asked.

Unexpected Consequences of Watching TV

But she had some misgivings, so she always stayed close by while he was watching and limited his viewing to a few shows with good lessons to teach—like *Sesame Street* and *Thomas and Friends*—which she recorded for him to watch when it best fit her schedule. He particularly liked Thomas the Tank Engine, whose adventures he quickly learned to reconstruct with his interlocking blocks train set.

Gray couldn't help noticing, however, that despite the powerful lessons about relationships and caring taught in these programs, Loren gravitated toward the spectacular and violent. When Thomas would occasionally get into a train wreck and spill all the milk in his tank cars, Loren took great delight in reenacting the accident with his interlocking blocks—pulling out one of the pieces just at the right moment and shouting with glee at the wreck he'd engineered on the family room floor.

On the one hand, Gray found herself amused by the intensity of his concentration, his quick hand movements, the imitative sounds he made, and his sheer joy in imaginative play. On the other hand, it worried her. On the screen, of course, even Thomas's most horrendous mix-ups ended happily; on the carpet too, the blocks quickly got reassembled. But real-life accidents, she knew, have real-life consequences that are anything but funny. How could she explain the nature of accidents to Loren—or should she even try? Her husband reminded her that there are only so many ways to make a show about trains exciting, and a train wreck is one of them. Still, it bothered her.

What Gray saw playing out on her carpet, however simple it seemed, was a situation with roots as ancient as they are complex. Since the first crowd on earth assembled, violence and calamity have apparently proved capable of seizing people's attention. At times that interest generates a compassionate, helpful, and well-meaning response to another's misfortunes. But just as often, it seems, the impulse degenerates into gossip, voyeurism, and a fascination with disaster. The earliest manifestations of theater capitalized on that appeal. In ancient Roman theater, slaves or condemned men were sometimes substituted at the last minute for actors whose script called for them to be murdered—and were then actually killed on stage. Audiences, sadly enough, were riveted by the spectacle and hurried back for more.

In recent decades, the rapid development of cinematic special effects has proved equally enticing, usually focusing more strongly on recreating gruesome details than on portraying noble values. The allure of adversity even colors our educational efforts, sometimes at the highest levels. Schools of medicine long ago recognized that a graphic depiction of wounds, diseases, and deformities gets the attention of students much more readily than pictures of normal, healthy tissues and organs.

Had Gray chosen to address Loren's absorption with debacles, would she have found herself fighting against the whole history of the human condition? Should she have accepted his behavior with a boys-will-be-boys shrug? Or were there some fundamental values

at stake, right there among the plastic blocks, that she needed
to address?

How Parents Can Control Media Use—and
Why They Should

According to recent research on how kids interact with modern
media, neither Gray's actions nor her doubts were misplaced. She's
not alone in falling back on TV as a babysitter. A 2006 survey of
American parents by the Kaiser Family Foundation spelled out
these statistics:

- On a typical day, 83 percent of children under the age
  of six use some form of screen media (TV, video or
  DVD, video games, and computers).

- Well over half of all babies one year old or younger
  spend an average of eighty minutes a day in front of
  TVs or computers.

- In many households, TV is a constant presence—
  always there, always on, and playing in the kitchen,
  dining room, family room, and bedrooms.

Among children Loren's age—the two and three year olds—
researchers made these discoveries:

- Most can turn on the TV by themselves (82 percent)
  or change channels with the remote (54 percent), and
  a large minority (42 percent) can already put in a
  DVD or video by themselves.

- On average, children this age spend one hour fifty-one
  minutes using screen media each day—well beyond
  the time spent playing outside (one hour twenty-six

minutes) or reading or being read to (forty-two minutes).

- Nearly 30 percent of children in this age cohort have a TV in their bedroom.

Asked why parents give children their own TVs, more than half explain that it frees up other TVs in the house so they can watch their own shows. Other reasons include the one Gray cited: nearly 40 percent say they use screen media to keep the child occupied so they can do other things. They also mention that it helps the child fall asleep (30 percent) and they use it to reward good behavior (26 percent). As a California parent told Kaiser researchers, "Media makes life easier. We're all happier. He isn't throwing tantrums. I can get some work done."

Still, parents remain suspicious. A 2007 survey from the Pew Research Center found that nearly four in ten Americans (38 percent) listed "societal factors" when asked to name "the biggest challenge for parents today." Among the top three issues on that list were the impact of television and other media. Their instinct squares with grave concerns expressed by the American Academy of Pediatrics (AAP), which recommends that children under two years old not watch any TV at all. Neurological research suggests that the first two years of life are critical to brain development and that screen media can cut into the time children need for play, exploration, and relationship building with adults and other children. Some studies suggest that media violence promotes real-life violence, though that conclusion remains in dispute. Less disputable is the research suggesting that early immersion in a video culture contributes to attention problems as teens.[9] Citing recent studies from New Zealand, a 2007 report from the AAP found that "for every additional 50 minutes of television watched on average per day, there was a measurable negative impact on attention." Why? Possibly because, according to the report, "the world portrayed on television makes real-life tasks seem boring in comparison"—or because "watching TV displaces the activities that encourage attention, such as reading and playing games." Or perhaps there's a more physiological basis. Summarizing the latest findings on the neurobiological basis of morality, researcher Darcia Navaraez observes that the prefrontal cortex—that part of the brain associated with orchestrating thought and action in accordance with internal goals—may be damaged by "behavior choices such as binge drinking and violent video game playing, which suppress activation of the prefrontal cortex even during normal problem solving, turning normal brains into ones that look like those of aggressive delinquents."[10]

While Loren seems in little danger of becoming an aggressive delinquent, should Gray nevertheless stop him from watching? Is she at risk of becoming a media-lenient parent, in the words of the 2010 media study we reported in Chapter One? Or is she helping Loren to interact more broadly with the world? A balanced review of the issue, assembled by reporters for KidsHealth, a Web site sponsored by the Nemours Foundation, finds that "television, in moderation, can be a good thing: Preschoolers can get help learning the alphabet on public television, grade schoolers can learn about wildlife on nature shows, and parents can keep up with current events on the evening news."[11] It's an argument seconded by many of the parents who spoke to researchers from the Kaiser Family Foundation. "My daughter knows . . . her letters from *Sesame Street*," reported the mother of a preschooler. "I haven't had to work with her on them at all." Another mother noted that "out of the blue one day my son counted to five in Spanish. I knew immediately that he got that from *Dora*."

But other parents—even those who let their kids watch TV—have different views. "My daughter just sits in the beanbag chair watching TV," the mother of a daughter in the four-to-six-year-old cohort told the Kaiser researchers. "If it's something that she's really into, she just sits there with her mouth hanging

Teaching Good TV Habits

If you decide to let very young children watch TV, use the opportunity to help them develop good TV habits. An article on the KidsHealth Web site suggests the following ways to move TV from a surrogate babysitter to a more productive element of your parenting:

- *Provide "nonscreen entertainment" opportunities* in the room where the TV is located—books, toys, puzzles—to "encourage kids to do something else."
- *"Keep TVs out of bedrooms,"* and turn them off at mealtime.
- *"Treat TV as a privilege"* rather than a right, which kids earn by good behavior or after doing simple chores like neatening up.
- *"Set a good example* by limiting your own TV viewing."
- *"Preview programs* before your kids watch them."
- *"Watch TV together.* If you can't sit through the whole program, at least watch the first few minutes to assess the tone and appropriateness, and then check in throughout the show."
- *"Talk to kids about what they see on TV,* and share your own beliefs and values." Use good examples—and bad examples—as a source of conversation. "'Do you think it was okay when those men got in that fight? What else could they have done? What would you have done?'"
- *"Offer fun alternatives to television.* Suggest that you all play a board game, start a game of hide-and-seek, play outside, read, work on crafts or hobbies, or listen and dance to music."[12]

open." Another admitted, "It makes life easier now, but in the long run, when they're older and starting to run into all these problems, I think I'll wish I wouldn't have let them do it when they were five."

This last comment raises a warning cautiously voiced in the research community. As the Kaiser report concludes, "There has been very little research about the impact of media on the youngest children, especially those 2 years and under. Given how much a part of children's lives these media are, it seems important to explore in greater depth the impact media may be having on their development."[13]

What Does "Moral" Mean?

The Kaiser report's warning helps explain why Gray finds herself in such a moral quandary. A *moral* quandary? Indeed it is. The word *moral* points to distinctions between right and wrong—good and bad if you're focusing on behavior, or good and evil if you're thinking in religious terms. We use it today to mean one of two things. It can be a synonym for *right* or *good*, as in the comment, widely attributed to George Washington, that "happiness and moral duty are inseparably connected." Or we use it to describe issues that deal with matters of right and wrong, as when President John F. Kennedy, referring to the question of "whether we are going to treat our fellow Americans as we want to be treated," noted that in this question "we are confronted primarily with a moral issue."[14] Granted, the word has been poisoned by its association with *moralizing*, which runs all the way from a tedious spouting of aphorisms to cocksure lecturing by those who find fault with others. The word has also been warped by a confusion of morality with sexual probity. In the 1950s euphemism, a man hauled into court on "a morals charge" was not going to be tried for beating his children or defrauding his neighbors (though those are clearly immoral acts), but specifically for engaging in sexual misconduct. In Gray's case, the moral question she faced was neither a temptation to moralize nor a concern with sexual impropriety. It was moral because it raised questions of right and wrong in her role as a parent.

How is she to think this through? Once again, the five core values can provide a starting point. Knowing the importance of responsibility, she may conclude that when she has a strong opinion on something—in this case, her concern for Loren's fascination with Thomas and his train wrecks—she has a duty to communicate it. Knowing the importance of honesty and truth telling, she may feel less than candid if she doesn't address the issue with him. Loren, she knows, is smart. Will he sense from her an implied criticism of his playtime antics despite her smiles and amusement? Is it best to find a way, even at that early age, to voice her concerns to him? Might she, using the simplest language about respect for others, help him build a little village beside the train tracks where his best friend lives—and ask him to imagine how that friend would feel if his dog got hurt in the wreck? If Loren is causing an accident just for fun, is that fair to his friend—and loving to his dog? Does Loren want to be the cause of disasters that harm others? Or would he rather be a hero who takes responsibility for preventing them?

Gray may decide not to engage with Loren in this way because she feels he's not yet able to comprehend such things, or because her husband may have a differing view, or because she doesn't want to stifle her son's TV watching creativity as an imaginative participant rather than a couch potato. But whether she actually speaks to Loren about it, the very act of working out what she might say gives her valuable practice in articulating an ethical argument—clarifying her moral reasoning and sharpening her values. By recognizing that she faces a moral choice and taking the time to apply her values to help her think through her options, she's laying the groundwork for future conversations around a moral question as old as humanity and as fresh as a two year old's laugh.

Lessons from

Loren Wrecks the Train

- Even simple activities like playing with blocks can raise ethical issues. As you become more ethically aware, you will spot opportunities for lessons that many other parents will never see.
- "Just because everyone does it doesn't make it right." Someday you'll say that to your teenagers. So apply it to yourself: Is TV watching "right" just because it makes your own life easier?
- You can develop your ethical fitness by thinking through every situation that makes you morally uncomfortable, even if you never talk to your child about it.

Ages Five Through Nine

It's a setting repeated across America's exurbs: the one-chair hair salon in the split-level ranch house, the separate grade-level entrance, and the modest sign planted in the front yard and rooted in a pun—*Hair We Are*, or *Shear Delight*, or *Comb On In*. You can read its history at a glance. It's owned and operated by a thirty-something hairstylist who worked downtown for years. Her loyal and flattering clientele have increasingly wrenched around their schedules to get on her calendar. The childhood years of her own kids have been flashing by far too fast—especially during after-school hours when her schedule has been heaviest, and she has longed to be home. She's got a craving for a better work-life balance. She's also got a handyman husband to fit out the basement with mirrors and track lights—and a lot of gnawing doubts about inconveniencing her clients with longer drive times and a shift from metro chic to suburban simple. But at last comes the decision, the plunge, the gulp—and the amazement when, having built it, they come.

Teaching Thrift in an Age of Opulence

It was a pattern Chrissie followed almost to the letter when she made such a move not long ago in downstate Illinois. Yes, it was a hard transition—and yes, it was scary. But in the end, the interruptions from thirteen-year-old Josh and eight-year-old Penny during late-afternoon appointments—"Can I go to the movie tonight?" "Can you brush my hair into a ponytail before the soccer game?"—were minor compared to her newfound flexibility. She and Will, her husband, still had a significant juggling act each day to keep up with their kids' after-school activities. But her customers were impressed by her commitment to active child raising. They understood that Josh and Penny were seeing basic business etiquette at work every day in their own basement: frugality, service, promise keeping, skillfulness, and the dozens of other traits without which small businesses fail.

So when Penny began lobbying for a shopping trip to Limited Too, a clothing chain in a nearby mall popular with her third-grade friends at school, it was in Chrissie's nature to hold back. In part, she was appalled at the prices. She was also concerned that Penny was beginning to play the let-me-shop-with-my-pals card more persistently than she'd ever played it before. Yet Chrissie knew how much it meant to her daughter to keep up with her friends and be part of the group. Chrissie's own upbringing—she'd been one of three children in a low-income, single-parent home—had taught her to appreciate what she had and be happy with it. Those values had contributed strongly to her entrepreneurial success, and she wanted Penny to learn that same appreciation. Yet she was hugely grateful that her daughter hadn't had to go through the experience of penury, and she didn't want to impose it on her artificially out of a "what was good enough for me is good enough for you" mind-set.

Chrissie saw the rightness of standing firm against unwise expenditures. She longed to draw out the lessons of self-restraint in the face of advertising and independence in response to peer pressure. But she wondered whether that was making a mountain out of a molehill. Was Penny's fascination with that store merely a passing fancy that would leave no damaging habits in its wake? Was the whole thing so petty and immaterial that any resistance on Chrissie's part could endanger something much more valuable: a mother-daughter relationship she had just moved heaven and earth (and a hair salon) to nurture and develop? What was she to do?

Finding the Middle Ground Between Permissive and Authoritarian

Chrissie was facing the choice every parent encounters between authority and accommodation, firmness and acceptance, short-leash restrictiveness and long-leash guidance. She was up against the tension created by demandingness and responsiveness. Those two core concepts underlie the work of American developmental psychologist Diana Baumrind. In research dating from 1966, Dr. Baumrind described parental responsiveness as the degree to which a parent responds to a child's needs. Parental demandingness, by contrast, indicated the extent to which a parent requires of a child an increasing sense of responsibility and unselfishness. High-demanding parents with little responsiveness she called *authoritarian*, while low-demanding parents who are highly responsive she called *permissive*. Between them are the demanding but responsive parents whom, somewhat confusingly, she labeled *authoritative*. In the large body of research generated over forty years by what's now called Baumrind's typology, her fourth combination—where parents neither demand nor respond—is called either *neglecting-rejecting* or simply *unengaged*. Her system is laid out visually in Figure 3.1.

As Baumrind argued and subsequent research confirms, the best parenting comes from the authoritative group in the upper-right corner. They seem to strike the proper balance between the demanding and the responsive. Firm and consistent, they are also warm and supportive. They have high levels of reasoning and sensitivity coupled with a commitment to nurture the autonomy of their offspring. Not surprisingly, they get the best long-term results. Among other measures, study after study confirms that their children have higher academic performance than those from other quadrants.[1]

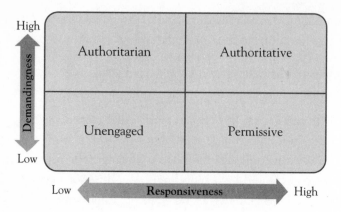

Figure 3.1 Baumrind's Typology

If these parents ramp up their demandingness, tamp down their responsiveness, and shift into the authoritarian quadrant at the upper left, they become more controlling, power asserting, and rejecting. They can end up with a rigid, harsh, "my way or the highway" directiveness. Taken to extremes, the authoritarian mind-set becomes abusive. Parents who slip down into the permissive quadrant at the lower right become soft, indulgent, and lax. Upholding neither rules nor guidelines for their children's behavior, they take an indifferent, hands-off stance toward discipline. And if they drop down into complete disengagement—neither responsive nor demanding—research suggests that their children tend to grow up to be "significantly more nonconforming, maladjusted, dominating, selfish, and unoriginal," along with having "a higher consumption of alcohol than children from most other homes."[2]

To Chrissie, as to many other nonspecialist readers, these findings are intuitively obvious. She could probably find in households in her neighborhood examples to confirm that an unyielding rigidity produces results just as bad as an anything-goes laxity. What's more, Josh and Penny would find it just as easy to identify children from permissive homes—the so-called spoiled kids—as they would the insecure and unhappy kids from authoritarian households. The usefulness of this research, then, is not simply that it confirms what parents instinctively feel. It's that it reinforces the sense that the best parenting occupies a middle ground of moderation between demandingness and responsiveness.

Justice Versus Mercy

Baumrind's typology aligns, in a way, with the justice-versus-mercy paradigm for ethical decision making. The demands imposed by justice and principle must constantly be weighed against the responsiveness elicited by mercy and compassion. Not surprisingly, some of the toughest dilemmas in parenting are generated along this demand-response, justice-mercy axis. That's where Chrissie found herself as she addressed Penny's foray into Limited Too. In her case, she was able to negotiate a middle way that let her have something of both sides. When Penny received a birthday gift card, Chrissie let her top it up with some money she had saved. Penny was then able to buy a single outfit for eighty dollars. Since the clothing was essentially a gift, Chrissie treated it as a one-off exception that didn't compromise her ongoing strategy of helping Penny learn the value of thrift. As for Penny, since her mother had let her buy something she wanted, she felt pleased and successful. Yet Chrissie couldn't help noticing that her influence must have seeped through to Penny. The trip to Limited Too, far from launching an unstoppable freight train of desire for more and more costly outfits, seemed to have put to rest Penny's fascination with that store. She never again begged to be taken there.

What Chrissie had found was a classic trilemma option: a middle way through the horns of her justice-versus-mercy dilemma. As a resolution, it extracted the best of each side. Because her mother didn't capitulate to her request at the outset, Penny's growing sense of the importance of thrift was reinforced.

But because Chrissie saw this situation as an exception, she was able to invoke the "just this once" argument and allow Penny to do what she most wanted at the time. Left behind was the authoritarianism sometimes suggested by the word *justice* and frequently accompanied by phrases like "No, never!" or "Over my dead body!" Left behind, too, was the permissiveness that could have said, "I love Penny, so I need to let her do whatever she wants." Although not every dilemma has a trilemma option —a point explained more fully in Chapter Five, "Finding the Third Way"—the trilemma seemed by far the best solution in this case.

But the real test facing Chrissie during those years came not from the tastes and desires of Penny's peers. It came from a seemingly unlikely source: Penny's grandmother. After years of raising children on shoestring budgets, Chrissie's mom had remarried late in life and now found herself able to provide things for her grandchildren she could never have given her own children. That pattern of lavish giving was particularly noticeable at the elaborate Christmas festivities she hosted each year, replete with a glut of gifts that her grandchildren may have wanted but certainly didn't need. Was it a real generosity or simply an excessive opulence?

Barbie Versus Feminism

Over the years, Jillian and her husband, Lon, have made a special point of helping their children understand the pull of consumerism and the trap ("We refer to *the trap* a lot," she says) that is laid to make them feel they simply must have the latest toy or gadget to be happy. Jillian and Lon want them to understand that it's not the car or the house—or the toy—that produces this desire. The allure comes from the culture in which they live, which says that happiness comes from external things.

Jillian is particularly sensitive to marketing that portrays women in an unrealistic and sexualized manner, teaching even little girls to think of themselves as objects rather than individuals. So when eight-year-old Robin begged for a Barbie doll, almost the first words out of Jillian's mouth, she recalls, were, "Absolutely not! We don't do Barbies in our house!"

Through the tears and protests that followed, Jillian did her best to explain her reasons for saying no. To each objection, however, the persistent Robin responded by reassuring her mother: she would never wear lots of makeup, she would love herself just the way she was, she would still think of herself as beautiful, and she would never wiggle her bottom when she walked like Barbie did on TV. Jillian began to wonder if she shouldn't let Robin have a Barbie—until she remembered that she really didn't like Barbies and didn't want to support the Barbie industry.

So she was very grateful when a third option occurred to her and the dilemma turned into a trilemma. She gave Robin a piggy bank and explained that she could buy the Barbie herself if she earned the money. In under a month, Robin had done all kinds of extra jobs around the house for pay— learning, Jillian felt, something of the value of money and the virtue of persistent work—and she took Robin to the store to buy her Barbie. As a goodwill gesture, Jillian even chipped in for an extra outfit.

The lesson for Jillian? "You can't do good parenting or good teaching if you're always thinking only from within your own shoes," she points out. Robin understood her concerns and still made a reasonable decision to buy a Barbie—even if it was different from Jillian's own, reasonable decision not to support the Barbie mystique.

For a while, Chrissie tried to discourage her mother's indulgence, largely because she saw it undermining the values she herself was trying to instill in her children. But her mom was impervious to her pleas. The situation put Chrissie and her husband so much at loggerheads that for some years, Will refused to attend such family gatherings—though, as he came to understand how much Josh and Penny looked forward to these occasions and to being with their cousins, he ultimately relented.

Did Will wisely surrender? Or was this a cowardly capitulation? Should he have stood his ground to make a moral point about the abuse of money and the excesses of materialism? Or was he modeling for his children a quiet discretion and an exemplary unselfishness in putting his personal peeves aside for the sake of family harmony? In the context of our five core values, was he sustaining compassion and respect—but at the cost of abandoning responsibility, honesty, and fairness?

Given the pull and tug of forces acting on parenting these days, the question is probably unfair. "Parents are caught on the horns of a dilemma," writes Baumrind, in which children, "in order to become self-regulated, individuated, competent individuals," must be given both "freedom to explore and experiment" and a high degree of "protection from experiences that are clearly dangerous." She cites an "apt metaphor" from fellow psychologist Philip A. Cowan, who notes that in parenting, there is "rough terrain that must be crossed, risks that must be faced and surmounted," and that "the successful outcome of the journey is not assured."[3]

In the long seasons of their children's development, can parents negotiate this rough terrain by changing their locations in Baumrind's quadrant? Should parents of young children, needing what she calls the "protection from experiences that are clearly dangerous," be more demanding—perhaps even authoritarian—at early ages? Should they subsequently, as children mature, phase into a permissive mind-set that gives more mature children the "freedom to explore and experiment"? While that's a fine hypothesis, in practice it appears that parents don't shift their parenting style as children mature. Researchers Laura Weiss and Conrad Schwarz note that in theory, you might expect parents to "change their child-rearing strategy as their children mature." Thus, "parents who are highly autonomy-granting when the children are younger may be providing too much freedom, whereas parents who appropriately reduce direct control over their children in late adolescence may be helping their children to develop self-esteem and autonomy." In fact, these authors conclude, "Research evidence points to the contrary, namely, that both parents' and children's behaviors are relatively stable over time."[4] Although it may be too rigid to assert that "once an authoritarian, always an authoritarian," the research does suggest that parents lock into a style of parenting early in their children's lives that lasts a lifetime.

Why Authoritative Parents Best Promote Their Child's Moral Development

Of the three most common parenting approaches—authoritarian, authoritative, and permissive—which best promotes the moral development in children? Which produces the most ethical kids? Here the research is unanimous in favor of the middle ground of authoritative parenting. Is it because authoritative parents create an atmosphere of greater discussion? Do they simply talk a lot about ethics in general? Or do they consistently articulate key moral principles? An intriguing study by University of London researcher Patrick J. Leman, based on children in the London suburbs, examined parenting styles based on these differing models.[5] The study makes two basic assumptions. First, it assumes that by definition, authoritative parents invite dialogue and discussion (the responsiveness side of Baumrind's typology) while also insisting on rules to be followed (the demandingness side). Second, it assumes that authoritative parenting, as the research shows, creates more ethical offspring.

The question is, Why is this style most effective? Is it attributable to what Leman calls the "discursive atmosphere" of easy and open conversation in the home, which in and of itself promotes better moral development? Or is it that these parents offer what he describes as "specific justifications" that help children understand why they should act morally? Not surprisingly, his study suggests the latter. Authoritative parents aren't successful simply because they have more lively chats about ethics with their kids. They succeed because, during those talks, they help kids gravitate toward sounder moral positions.

In Lehman's experiments, when children asked their parents, "Why shouldn't I do this or that?" he found the following:

- Authoritarian parents were more likely to favor such responses as, "Because I said so," or "Because I make the rules."

- Permissive parents favored justifications based on the consequences for other children: "Because that would hurt her," or "Because you need to consider how she would feel if you did it." But, being permissive, they did not tend to enforce any moral rules.

- Authoritative parents, between those two extremes, favored responses based on a kind of rational equality between parent and child: "Because you wouldn't like it if I did it to you," or "Because I trust you."

In practice, all parents use a range of responses in moral discussions with their children. So this research seeks only to find trends rather than absolutes. We should also note that this study focuses on eleven year olds in school populations that were "broadly middle class and predominantly of white ethnic origin."[6] Finally, rather than asking parents how they actually responded, the study asked the children how they thought their parents would respond in various scenarios. Nevertheless, the research suggests that sound moral development may be "a consequence of parents communicating a specific content or type of moral rule rather than a consequence of any discursive atmosphere."[7] In other words, neither a loose chat about ethics nor a prim and moralizing seminar does as much for the moral development of the next generation as a lively interchange rooted in decided principles. Those who see a contradiction in this phrase ("How can a conversation about *principles* be *lively?*") have never seen how animated and engaged young people can become when their own principles are challenged—as the following stories suggest.

Lessons from

Teaching Thrift in an Age of Opulence

- Raising children tests the balance of parental demandingness versus responsiveness. Strive for the authoritative position that blends the two.
- Beware of extremes. Too much responsiveness—a soft, lax indulgence—can lead to an indifference toward discipline and rules. In the long run, permissive parenting is harmful.
- A controlling, power-asserting rigidity—the "my way or the highway" approach—arises from overweighting demandingness. This authoritarian style is unsuccessful.
- Parenting styles usually get fixed early on. Don't think you can start as an authoritarian and become more permissive as your children mature. Nice thought, but it won't happen.
- Discussion is vital. But ground it in principle. Saying, "Let's talk!" won't help unless you bring specific moral justifications to the table. Gabbing about ethical issues isn't enough.

Teaching Ethics Through Principles

Grant and his wife, Holly, both hold faculty positions at a leading American university in the South. Not surprisingly, perhaps, nine-year-old Daphne has been raised in a fully "discursive atmosphere." As Grant concedes, the default position in their household is to talk rather than stay silent, question rather than merely accept, and lead rather than lag. Their daughter, it seems, has taken all these attributes into her schooling. If not precocious, she is without a doubt fully engaged in her learning, with an intellectual maturity beyond her years and a passion for excelling. She's never had to be pushed. Success, academic and extracurricular, has been an unquestioned goal that seems to have come more or less naturally.

Yet Grant has noticed something else through the years. At first it seemed simply a matter of his daughter's difficulty in taking criticism—a kind of defensiveness, an unwillingness to be challenged, an inability to accede gracefully when she has made a mistake, a reluctance to apologize. But at times it has seemed more troubling. Sometimes a passing comment intended to correct a small detail had caused an explosive meltdown or a surly withdrawal, darkening the atmosphere and foreclosing further discourse. He has seen in Daphne a deep and competitive desire to please her highly educated parents—so much so that any suggestion that she has missed the mark seems tantamount, in her mind, to an accusation of total failure.

Daphne Reveals a Secret She Shouldn't

So Grant was torn when he heard about the party at Shannon's house. The gaggle of third-grade girls had been sitting in a circle playing telephone, that famously instructive game illustrating how a verbal message degrades with every retelling. It had been going along well enough, each round beginning with a girl whispering some phrase to her neighbor, who in turn whispered it to the next in line, until it returned along the circle to the teller in a form so distorted and exaggerated as to cause gales of laughter. When Daphne's turn came to initiate the whisper, she told the girl beside her that their mutual friend Wendy, who was part of the circle, still wore special diapers ("pull-ups," as Daphne called them) to prevent her from wetting her bed at night.

Grant never knew what happened next—whether Wendy, on hearing her inmost secret divulged, ran from the room in tears, or whether the tale was so corrupted as to be unintelligible when it reached her. The upshot, however, was a deeply offended rebuke from Wendy's parents. Hearing from some of the other girls at the party what Daphne had said, they sharply criticized Grant and Holly for raising such a child, saying they wanted nothing more to do with their family. When Grant confronted Daphne, she insisted she hadn't done it—and flipped into shutdown mode. From everything Grant had heard, he was certain that Wendy did indeed use pull-ups and that Daphne had said so.

What to do? Talking it over with his wife, he could see that a serious moral question was at stake. Wearing pull-ups was, after all, a deeply personal and embarrassing matter for any nine year old. How widely it was known among Wendy's friends, he didn't know. But that, he saw, wasn't the point. The canons of decent behavior, at least in the adult world, made it clear that such personal details should be left unspoken—even if they were widely known. Although he was surprised that Daphne didn't grasp that basic piece of decorum, a moment's reflection convinced him that at her age, there had been no opportunity to learn it. Yet in the world of social grace in which she would soon be moving, that kind of mature discretion would be essential. The incident was not something to be tossed lightly aside. Grant and Holly agreed that it needed to be handled immediately and powerfully—and that Daphne had done something very wrong.

How to Explain Why Something Is Wrong

Suppose, though, Daphne were to ask, "*Why* is it wrong? Is it just because you don't like it?" Here Grant could share with her the core moral values—honesty, responsibility, respect, fairness, and compassion—that he and Holly held in high regard and are widely understood to define the ethical life. They also define the reverse: that which is unethical is dishonest, irresponsible, disrespectful, unfair, or lacking in compassion. Here Grant might call Daphne's attention to the word *or*. It's not necessary, he might explain, to fail in all five categories in order to be doing something unethical. Surely a few well-aimed questions to Daphne would be in order. Which of the values had she upheld? She might point to honesty, since Wendy did wear pull-ups and she was only reporting the facts. She might also point to responsibility, since the game required her to participate, and it was her duty to think of a phrase that was potentially funny, even startling, to her friends. Where, then, had she drifted away from these core values? With a little thought, she would probably admit that she had been disrespectful of Wendy's dignity. She had been unfair in categorizing Wendy as someone babyish and lacking control, when in fact the state of her health was not of Wendy's own choosing. And she had been lacking in compassion in mocking Wendy's suffering, when true friendship would call forth sympathy and affection.

Grant might also have turned to the five well-tried tests for wrongdoing that Daphne could use. Whenever she finds herself facing a choice between A and B—in this case, to use this story in the game or to find another—she can ask, "Are both of these choices ethical, or is this a choice between right and wrong?" A quick look at the following tests makes the point:

- *The legal test.* Does either A or B break the law? No. The law is generally silent on what nine year olds whisper at slumber parties.

- *The regulations test.* Would either A or B break any explicit rules? Probably not. If this had been a board game or a round of cards, with clearly stated rules governing the play, it would have been wrong to knowingly break a rule. But in this sort of parlor game, rules are rarely written down or recited aloud before play begins.

- *The stench test.* Does one side or the other just stink? From Grant's point of view, this intuitional, gut-feeling test raised all sorts of warning flags. Lacking his maturity and social sensitivity, however, Daphne blew right past this one in a way that she might never have done a few years later.

- *The front-page test.* Would Daphne be comfortable if the whole story appeared on the front page of tomorrow morning's newspaper, whether it was about A or B? If it were headlined, "Nine Year Old Outs Diaper-Wearing Classmate," she might well be horrified.

- *The Mom test.* Could she imagine her mom—or some other moral exemplar she admires greatly as a good person—telling on Wendy in this way? This last test is probably the most relevant. Would either Grant or Holly have whispered something like this about one of their friends—or about her? If they wouldn't, why should she?

Conceptually, then, Grant has plenty of ways to let Wendy know that she's made a serious mistake. But knowing someone has done wrong is very different from explaining the wrongdoing so effectively that a life is reformed. How was Grant to cut through Daphne's predictable meltdown when he pointed out her failing? If he had been inclined toward permissiveness, he would have sheltered Daphne with great responsiveness while making few, if any, demands. Had he been an authoritarian, he might have rolled like a bulldozer over her feelings, insisting on public apologies and warning her never to say such things again. In fact, he chose a middle ground. The principle that needed to be applied, he saw, was the Golden Rule, which asked Daphne to put herself in Wendy's position and imagine how it would feel to have someone say that kind of thing about her. But he also needed to find a way to telegraph to Daphne that she was not a failure in his eyes. Somehow he needed to help her see that he could understand what lay behind her initial whisper.

Explaining Why Jokes Can Hurt

Oddly enough, he found that way through levity. He began the conversation by agreeing that in some abstract way that involved potty humor, the picture of an almost adolescent in diapers was, well, *funny*. He told her he could see how, innocently enough, she could have thought such a tale might be witty and amusing among her friends. While he admitted to me that he had not been fully comfortable using this approach, he felt he had to let her know he wasn't accusing her of being deliberately mean. He hastened to tell her, however, that such a joke would almost certainly be—as jokes so often are—cruel and hurtful. The important thing, he pointed out, was not the ability to tell a joke, but the ability to care for others, understand their feelings and sensitivities, and help build them up rather than tear them down. Surely, he argued, she would want Wendy to do that for her. So she needed to do it for Wendy as well.

Much to his relief, Daphne responded to this line of reasoning. Her reaction didn't come as an immediate softening; their discussion was still earnest on his side and sullen on hers. But in a remarkably short time, Daphne rallied, understood her obligations, and rendered a sincere apology for her actions. There was still some lingering bitterness on the part of Wendy's parents. But Grant felt Daphne had confronted this issue for what it was—not as a merely social circumstance or as an instance of the who's-in and who's-out politics so dominant at her age, but as a fundamentally ethical question. She comprehended the need to remedy her mistake by applying one of the three resolution principles—the Golden Rule—that have served humanity for centuries as reliable guides to moral development.

How Grant addressed the issue confirms, in a small way, the research about parenting styles. What moved Daphne forward in her journey of moral development was not simply a discursive atmosphere, which seemed hard to establish in the current context of intensity. The effect came from a specific justification—Grant's willingness to describe and apply a clear set of moral values and a defined moral rule (in this case, the Golden Rule) to this situation. Improvement came, he felt, not simply because he and his daughter talked, but because they talked in a particular way about a distinct moral proposition, and because Grant was able to couple the responsiveness of humor to the demand for adherence to a rule.

Lessons from   Teaching Ethics Through Principles

- The simplest circumstance can raise a profound ethical issue. Don't overlook it just because it started as a party game. Seize the moment, and make the point.
- An unethical act is dishonest, irresponsible, disrespectful, unfair, *or* lacking compassion. Emphasize the *or*; failing in any one category is enough to warrant the label *unethical*.
- Kids need tests for telling right from wrong. Walk them through the five steps—laws, regulations, stench, front page, and Mom—and let them discover where they went wrong.
- As a parent, there's a world of difference between knowing what's right and explaining right winningly. Your key job is to find ways to say the unpleasant effectively.

Ethics and Peer Pressure

Late one afternoon, Sharon found an elegant, handsomely bound, and obviously expensive book of fairy tales tucked away in a pocket of her second-grade daughter's backpack. Sharon hadn't been prying. She hardly ever opened Sylvie's backpack. But Sylvie had left it in the kitchen when she came home from school that day, and Sharon had something she wanted to put in it before school the next day. Sharon had never seen the book before, and she was pretty sure it didn't belong to Sylvie. When Sylvie came back into the kitchen, there it lay on the table. Within moments, a bawling and distraught second grader admitted that she had stolen it from the school book fair two weeks earlier.

The Stolen Book

Reflecting later, Sharon realized that she'd had several courses of action open to her that day. Without thinking, however, she found herself following a pattern she recognized as coming straight from her own childhood and her own mother. Lapsing into questions that were really accusations, she demanded to know how Sylvie could have done such a thing. How could she be a member of *this* household and do something *that* bad and *that* dishonest? Did she have any idea of how it made her parents feel? These were, of course, unanswerable questions, especially for a weeping second grader who had already confessed, and Sharon immediately wished she'd taken a quieter approach. But the whole thing, she said, had been an affront to her ego and an implicit criticism of her parenting. After all, what did it say about her own ability to communicate and instill ethics if this was to be the result? What's more, she was afraid—afraid for Sylvie's own uncertain moral compass, for her relationship with the school, and for what this little incident might be saying about her ability to navigate her ethical future.

"We had a really good time working *that* one out," Sharon told us. In the blowup, she came to see that Sylvie had been agonizing for two weeks about the book. She inherently knew she'd done something wrong; no one had to tell her that. She just didn't know how to solve the problem. The discomfort hit her every time she opened her backpack, and she longed to find a way out of it. Once Sharon saw that anguish and let go of her initial reaction, she said she "calmed down and realized that my job was to help Sylvie through this and not to punish her for it. She had already punished herself."

That didn't mean, however, that no restitution was needed. Together they arranged for Sylvie to meet with the principal, give him a letter of apology she had written, and talk about how she would pay for the book. In the process, however, something significant came to light: Sylvie had been goaded into taking the book by another student, a classmate who seemed to operate along that moral edge where creativity brushed up against irresponsibility. Always pushing the envelope, stopping just short of breaking the law, this little girl continually blurred the line where zany, imaginative fun topples over into dangerous or mean-spirited risk taking. What's more, she seemed to get satisfaction from influencing others to do what she herself never would do.

What to Do When Your Child Keeps Bad Company

What does a parent do in that circumstance? Sharon had strong concerns about the other's girl's moral stance, but she knew it fell to the principal and the administration, rather than to her, to address those issues. So she and Sylvie instead talked about the risk of being drawn into bad behavior. She was able to help Sylvie understand that she herself was a good person who knew right from wrong. She encouraged Sylvie to recognize that her core values were well established—that she was honest with herself, respectful of others' property, and responsible about owning up to mistakes. She was capable of doing her own thinking rather than simply doing what everyone else did. She could tell when the capers her friends planned bordered on impropriety, and she knew when the behaviors they actually exhibited were inappropriate. She also had the sense to know when her own behavior was off the mark—indeed, she had known immediately after taking the book that it wasn't right. What's more, she had already experienced the undermining, unsettling feeling of having done wrong and not knowing how to correct the theft. That very feeling was a strong signal that her moral sense was intact. Had she been void of values, she would have felt no remorse at all.

If Sharon had simply let the matter stand as she first addressed it—an explosion of fear and anger over the fact that Sylvie had stolen a book—she would have missed the opportunity to teach Sylvie an invaluable life lesson: the need to defend her own moral and mental standards from outside influences. Even as early as second grade, children can understand that a lot of forces are pulling on them, running all the way from peer pressure and old-fashioned backyard gossip right up to the latest forms of social media and the deliberately malicious influences of unethical classmates and friends. They can learn how to protect themselves from the subtle manipulations of others just as they learn to protect their physical property from those who appear to be friends but turn out to be thieves.

Spotting Childish Manipulators

Sharon can help Sylvie spot the manipulators by looking for these six signs:

- *Selfishness.* Is this friend thinking mostly about herself, or is she concerned about others? An unselfish friend builds relationships and helps you do better. A selfish friend seeks control and tries to use you for her own purposes.

- *Lack of commitment.* Does your friend really care about values, or is she uninterested in being honest, taking responsibility, and playing fair? If she's not committed to moral standards, she may resent your commitment to goodness and try to talk you out of it because you make her look bad.

- *Phoniness.* Is your friend a hypocrite who says one thing and does another, or is there a consistency between the appearance and the action? If your friend is open and transparent—not trying to hide things from you or from others—that's better than a friend who constantly promises and regularly fails to deliver.

- *Suspicion.* Is your friend usually suspicious of the motives of others, including you? Or is she trusting and forgiving? If she can't trust others, that's often a sign that she can't be trusted herself. But if she really cares about others, she'll usually give you the benefit of the doubt.

- *Excuse making.* Is your friend quick to explain away her bad behavior or to justify herself with complicated reasoning? She may be smart, but if she's good at using her intelligence to stretch the truth, she's also capable of giving you a less-than-accurate description of things—and deliberately deluding you.

- *Bragging.* Does your friend boast about her bravery, or is she genuinely courageous? She may talk a lot about her gutsy self-confidence, and even express it by taking dares and doing risky things. But does she have the moral courage to stand up for right and take action when her values are being tested?

A second grader may not always be successful in spotting these challenges. But neither are adults. All the more reason, then, for parents to help children recognize the nature of manipulation, cut through its disguises, and build up their moral defenses.

Lessons from

Ethics and Peer Pressure

- When kids know they've done some awful thing, and especially when they've confessed, keep your cool. The louder they get, the steadier you need to be.
- Confession doesn't let them off the hook. Good parenting responds, but it also makes demands. Apologies and restitution, especially to adults, help build character.
- Help children become good judges of character. They need to know which kids to trust, which to watch carefully but continue being with, and which to cut loose.
- Six warning signs alert kids to dangerous character: selfishness, lack of commitment, hypocrisy, suspicion, excuse making, and bravado. Help them spot these.

4

Ages Ten Through Fourteen

In *The Story of Doctor Dolittle* (1920), British author Hugh Lofting begins a series of now-classic children's books about a man who discovers how to talk to animals. On his trip to save monkeys in Africa, he comes across the pushmi-pullyu (pronounced *push-me-pull-you*), a timid hybrid of gazelle and unicorn with two heads, one at each end. Not surprisingly, when the creature tries to go somewhere, each head wants to make off in a different direction.

Although Dr. Dolittle has little to do with our discussion of ethical dilemmas, his imaginative beast reminds us of an important fact: unresolved dilemmas can paralyze us into immobility. And why not, since dilemmas are all about powerfully opposed forces? What's more, these forces act on us in different ways: what pulls you along, mentally and morally, may be exactly what pushes me away.

Resolving Ethical Dilemmas

How to help children reason through such dilemmas is a key parenting skill. But if you've sensed, thus far in the book, that making tough choices is not solely a matter of bedrock reasoning— that sometimes fundamental intuitions sweep in with an answer before we've even had time to formulate the question—you're onto something important. It's true that ethical dilemmas can present tricky, rational, pushmi-pullyu tugs-of-war. But it's also true that

they often trigger something within us that says, "Wait a minute—
this is the way forward." If we're asked why, we can usually give
sound, rational answers. But in our more candid moments, we have
to admit that sometimes the answer is, "Because it just feels right."

There's nothing shameful about that answer. In fact, argues
Harvard psychologist and biological anthropologist Marc D. Hauser,
that's the way we're built. "Moral dilemmas," he writes, "present us
with conflict, typically between two or more competing duties or
obligations. Confronted with such dilemmas, we deliver a judgment, a verdict of morally good or bad with respect to a person's
character or the act itself." While some of these judgments are well
reasoned, others "arise like flashes of lightning—spontaneous,
unpredictable, and powerful." Conflicts over our judgments
may occur, then, because "intuition and conscious reasoning have
different design specs." He continues:

> Intuitions are fast, automatic, involuntary, require little
> attention, appear early in development, are delivered
> in the absence of principled reasons, and often appear
> immune to counter-reasoning. Principled reasoning
> is slow, deliberate, thoughtful, requires considerable
> attention, appears late in development, [is] justifiable,
> and [is] open to carefully defended and principled
> counterclaims.[1]

Part of the work of moral parenting is to help children move
from their early-developing intuitions, which are often right,
to the kind of late-developing principled reasoning that is "open
to . . . counterclaims." First, however, we have to face up to our
own inner pushmi-pullyu—our own ever-present tension between
the intuitive and the rational. That doesn't mean one has to drive
out the other. True, the rationalist may smugly assert that while
half of Dolittle's beast was real—since there actually are gazelles
in Africa—the other half was a mere unicorn, known only to myth

and unseen in zoology. Therefore (the rationalist concludes), solid reason should trump fanciful intuition. The only problem with that logic is that our poor rationalist hasn't grasped the fact that we live in a world of balance. In a metaphor that Doolittle himself might have appreciated, moral parenting reminds us that if intuition without reason is a jellyfish, reason without intuition is a porcupine.

Is It Okay Not to Tell?

Lara had to face just such a dichotomy when she found her reason yanking her in one direction while her intuition wrenched her in the other. The question she faced was direct and stark: Is it ever right to tell only half a truth? Ordinarily she would have been the first to say no. As a manager of information technologies for a large corporation, she'd seen half-truths damage too many careers.

But then her son, Troy, turned eleven. When he was seven, Lara told me, he was diagnosed with a mild case of attention deficit disorder (ADD). With a doctor's advice, she and her husband put him on Ritalin. It "took the edge off," she recalled, "and helped him to concentrate."

Over the next four years, his energy seemed nothing more than a young boy's rambunctious creativity, so they saw no reason to change the original dosage even as his body grew. After four years and with a doctor's guidance, they pulled him off the drug for a summer. He was fine.

But as fall approached, Lara faced a tough choice. It wasn't about whether to go back to Ritalin; that, she felt, was behind them. It was about what to say to the teachers. He was heading into a new school where nobody knew his past. Should she divulge his medical history?

On the one hand, she felt she had a duty to tell. She and her husband strongly believed that "when you are dealing with the people who are educating your children, they need to understand your child." Only that way, she felt, can they "create environments where kids learn really well." Transparency, for them, was a deeply held value. She'd seen it bring significant improvements to her workplace simply by making openness and candor the standard mode of operation. In situations where information could legally be shared and where withholding it was not illegal, she felt things worked best when, absent a powerful reason for secrecy, the default position always said, *Share*. She had no doubt that in a school setting, transparency was just as important.

On the other hand, she felt an obligation to protect her son. She and her husband had fought hard to keep Troy from being stereotyped. She knew the danger of medical profiling. She knew the tendency of the mind to leap to conclusions about individuals, based on nothing more than a few apparent facts that seemed to match some vaguely formulated underlying assumptions. She knew, too, how quickly the mind charges into this process. "You read about people whose kids get labeled," she says, "and you say, 'I can't believe that happened so fast!' But children *do* get labeled pretty fast." She felt Troy had made significant progress and that he needed to be able to prove himself without any preconceptions.

Putting the Four Paradigms to Work

What Lara faced, in fact, falls right into the pool of light beneath our second lens: making tough choices. Hers was a classic right-versus-right decision, where the strongly held core value of honesty was coming directly into conflict with the equally powerful value of respect. Seen that way, she knew, there was no wrongdoing in sight—as our five tests for wrongdoing quickly confirm:

- She was not operating under a legal requirement to disclose or hide.

- There was no school regulation compelling her to divulge.

- She didn't detect any stench associated with either speaking up or remaining silent.

- Had her story appeared in the newspaper in full detail, she would have felt no shame in either explaining her son's medical history or seeking to shield him from a damaging label.

- She couldn't imagine her own mom—or a favorite uncle, a revered former teacher, or some highly regarded mentor at work—doing anything other than what she was doing.

She knew, in other words, that both sides were right. Yet she still had a choice to make: she couldn't both tell the school and not tell the school at the same time.

Lara found herself encountering a dilemma that was tough in four ways. It presented her with all four of our paradigms for understanding the tension that was tugging her both ways at once:

- Individual versus community

- Truth versus loyalty

- Short term versus long term

- Justice versus mercy

In Lara's case, the decision seemed first and foremost an individual-versus-community choice. It was clearly right to honor the educators, students, parents, and other community members who formed the broad social grouping known as "the school." It was easy to see that within broad limits, this community functioned best when it was communicating most actively and completely. That principle lies at the root of democracy: if everyone is to have an equal voice in the affairs of the community, then everyone needs equal access to the information relevant to the community. In this case, the relevant information had to do with creating a classroom climate free from disruption, inattention, or bad examples.

But it was equally right to defend her son's individuality. He was no mere cog in a wheel, but a fully formed expression of human dignity and respect, deserving recognition for his uniqueness and identity. That individuality, Lara could see, included a vigorous, active mentality. He was energetic and bright—qualities she regarded as a natural part of his being, not a disturbance to his character. He was determined to overcome any prior medical condition claiming abnormality or excessiveness. And she was determined to let him do so without allowing him to be labeled unfairly.

She was also facing the tension between truth and loyalty. While her own forthrightness made her cringe at misleading the school, her loyalty made her dread what she'd seen happen to other children with ADD. Truth would say, "Speak up," while loyalty would counter, "No, keep quiet." Yet the reasoning behind the truth-versus-loyalty paradigm could also have taken her in the opposite direction: she could have used the word *loyalty* to describe her long-standing commitment to work in close allegiance with the teachers, whereas what she saw as the nasty human penchant for labeling could have seemed to her to be the overriding truth in this situation.

Complicating the matter even further were the short-term-versus-long-term calculations. Should she, for the sake of an immediate, short-term benefit to her son—the benefit of having no one know his medical past—risk what might be a complicating, long-term downside if the ADD reasserted itself in damaging ways later in the year? Or should she sacrifice short-term happiness by creating what would no doubt be a harrowing and difficult year for him for the sake of buying long-term assurance that the problem was being addressed? While it was surely right in the long term to create a world of full disclosure, the short-term penalties for doing so seemed overwhelmingly severe.

Finally, what about justice versus mercy? If justice is all about our expectations and mercy all about our exceptions, Lara could have seen this as a special case lying outside the ordinary boundaries. Yes, it might be expected that parents would disclose everything to teachers—but in this case, surely she could have felt right invoking an exception. But was this such an exceptional case? She knew how easily the argument of exceptionalism can sweep through a parent's life—"He's not like any other child in the world. He's unique, and he deserves special treatment!"—and warp sound judgment and a sense of fairness. Did he deserve different treatment, or was this a fairly standard case?

How was Lara to decide? Notice how, in this analysis of the dilemma, we're produced a broad array of different arguments. But also notice that they fall naturally into two groups: those that say, "Tell all!" and those that say, "Keep still!" Imagine that Lara had a tabletop in front of her, with two stacks before her under two labels: one with all of the arguments for telling and the other with all of the counterarguments for not telling. Her job, in applying the paradigms, was not to come up with the most curious, bizarre argument anyone has ever heard and use it as the basis for her choice. No, her goal—the goal of any parent in this kind of situation—was simply to make each stack as tall as possible and then ask, "Which stack is higher?"

That last question is, of course, not quite fair. She's not going to get out her yardstick and measure her arguments by the inch. In this case, "higher" doesn't mean literally taller but figuratively more exalted: she's talking metaphorically, not geometrically. What she's looking for is the moral high ground. The ruler is not marked off in inches. It measures the applicability of a set of resolution principles that will allow her to say, "This side feels to me more right, more ethical, more correct." What she needs is some assurance that her decision, whichever way it goes, will be fully ethical.

Resolving Dilemmas: Three Principles

This lens also brings into view three resolution principles that appear to account for a great majority of decisions that parents describe as ethical:

- *Ends-based principle.* Known among philosophers as utilitarian thinking, it argues for doing the greatest good for the greatest number. Children and parents have long heard this principle articulated in the phrase, "Do what's best for everyone." If you're an ends-based thinker, the consequences, results, or ends of your action will determine its moral worth. Under this principle, if things turn out well for Troy, Lara could rest assured she had done the right thing— whereas if everything went south, she would have to admit she had made a terrible choice. Under an ends-based principle, then, her decision making would be based on a careful analysis of alternative futures and an effort to foresee all possible outcomes. Thinking about the greatest number by which to multiply her sense of the greatest good, she would quickly have seen that the category of *other children* would greatly exceed the category of *my family*. But she would also see that the harm done to one person (her son) by telling everyone else (the school) could be severe, immediate, and long term, while the potential harm to other children caused by her not telling would be modest at best, perhaps even negligible. Would an enormous harm to one person be greater than a minimal harm multiplied across a great number? Under this utilitarian calculus, she could certainly argue for refusing to tell.

- *Rule-based principle*. This standard urges parents to follow whatever action they would like to see universalized into an invariable precedent. Drawn from Immanuel Kant's "categorical imperative," this principle appears in every child's experience when a teacher says, "Johnny, if I let *you* do that, I'd have to let *everybody* do it." The question for Lara is this: Is there a rule I'd like everyone in the world to follow in similar circumstances? As a mother, she believed in the virtues of transparency and truth telling. As a corporate executive, she understood the need for managers—or, in this case, the teaching staff at Troy's school—to have access to all relevant information. So perhaps the rule should be, "Always tell the truth, regardless of the consequences." Under this rule-based approach, what determines morality is the motive, the rule, the universal obligation underlying the action. Get that right, Kant argued, and no matter how it turns out, you will have done the right thing. Following the rule-based principle, Lara could argue that a world where all parents withhold significant data about their children will, in the long run, be far inferior to a world where such information is candidly shared. Yes, the damage to her son might be significant. But, she could argue, this is about something much larger than my son. This is about truth itself. Under this principle, then, she may well be disposed to tell.

- *Care-based principle*. Widely known as the Golden Rule, this principle reminds parents to do to others what we would like to have others do to us. Not uniquely Christian or even specifically biblical, it lies at the heart of most cultures and religions around the world. Most of today's generation of parents, in fact, first encountered it somewhere in kindergarten when the teacher said something like, "Freddie, how would *you* feel if Kimmy hit *you* with that ruler?" This principle invokes a criterion of reversibility, where you mentally change places and look at the world through someone else's eyes. If "doing to others" means "doing to my child," parents can put themselves in the child's shoes and ask what the child would want them to do. But what if "others" means the teachers, or the child's best friend's mom, or the kid at the other end of a MySpace connection? If I were the teacher (Lara might say), of course I'd want full disclosure. But if I were Troy, I'd want to be protected from false profiling. This principle allows Lara to argue for either side—though probably, since most Golden Rule applications in practice identify "the other" as someone close to you and in immediate distress, Lara would have defined "the other" as Troy.

As Lara's case demonstrates, these three principles often provide conflicting answers. Here, one principle pulls her toward truth telling and the community's needs. Another draws her toward loyalty and the individual. The third could take her either way. In the end, Lara's decision will be based on what strikes her as the highest right. She may arrive at that conclusion through immediate intuition or deep moral reasoning. In either case, however, these resolution principles will help her toward a new clarity and confidence in her decision making, and toward an ability to explain the grounds of her decision to others so well that they can say, if they must, "Well, I don't agree with your decision, but I can't deny that you made an ethical choice."

How Lara Solved Her Dilemma

So what did Lara do?

After weighing both sides of this dilemma, she told me, she and her husband made a "conscious decision" to say nothing about the ADD. Early in the school year, Lara went to her first parent-teacher conference and was delighted by the "glowing results" she heard from the teacher. Troy was doing well in class, said the teacher, adding that "his grades are good, and we love having him here."

Lara was so pleased, she said, that she admitted to the teacher that they had taken Troy off Ritalin that summer. And that's where everything changed. As the words came out of her mouth, she recalls, she could see an immediate change come over the teacher's face—suddenly, unbelievably, and tragically. The teacher, Lara recalls, "shook her head and said, 'Oh, *now* I understand why I'm having so many problems with your son!'" From that point forward, Troy was, she says, "immediately labeled." For the rest of that year, Lara received a steady stream of notices about his performance issues, and "everything went downhill."

To this day, Lara told us, "I'm convinced that she just decided to label him. It didn't matter whether he was just being a typical kid. In her mind he *wasn't* being typical, he was 'that kid with ADD who needs to get on his medication again.'"

The next year, Troy changed schools. And since that episode, Lara admits, "I have not told the school system a thing." Troy is aware of his challenge, she added, and occasionally tells her that he's had a tough time concentrating, and they talk about it. But she says he's learning to handle it without drugs. "It was a tough fight going forward," she concludes.

But was it an *ethical* fight? Was this a wise defense of his dignity—or a willful disobedience of educational expectations? That depends on how you see the moral arguments on both sides. Some would say Lara did what every parent should do: take a firm stand against the all-too-human tendency, even among well-meaning educators, to see stereotypes instead of individuals. Others would say that every parent must share medical details with teachers—and that ethics depends less on how things turn out (fine, in this case) than on the principle (in this case, full disclosure) you'd like to see everyone follow.

In real life, of course, the decision will be determined by far more influences than we can ever capture in a few pages of analysis. An entire lifetime of relationship building, observation, and nuance will play into the choice. But with this set of tools at hand, even the toughest of dilemmas—and this surely was one—will be amenable to analysis, resolution, and explanation. With these frameworks in place, you'll be able to say at the end of the day, "I think I did the right thing, and here's why." Few things in parenting are more satisfying than that.

Lessons from

Resolving Ethical Dilemmas

- As kids develop, intuition usually precedes reason—and the two often push and pull in opposite directions. Parents can help their children find the proper balance.
- Sometimes it's right not to tell everything to everyone—which is not the same as speaking in half-truths. Candor is admirable, but so is discretion.
- Take time to analyze the situation in detail, and use the four paradigms. They help clarify the toughest of choices and show what you're up against.
- Remember that analysis is not resolution, and that the three resolution principles—ends based, rule based, and care based—help you either explain your intuitions or override them.

Zero Tolerance

In Lara's case, no body of law or regulation shaped her decision. It was, in many ways, a purely ethical choice. It wasn't quite so easy for John, who knew he had to make a phone call he really didn't want to make.

Arriving at his office early one Monday morning, he glanced across the lawn to the gym where Saturday night's prom had been held. Some years earlier, John had joined the staff of this independent day school for boys, honored to be part of a prestigious institution in a history-drenched midsized city. From the beginning, his duties as assistant headmaster included chaperoning the annual dance, held jointly with an equally well-regarded private school for girls across town.

Walking the halls at the prom that Saturday evening, John had had many brief, pleasant chats with students, most of whom he knew well. He particularly enjoyed running into Chase, a fourteen-year-old student leader with a quick wit and an easygoing friendliness. Not the absolute top of his class, not the captain of the football team, Chase was nevertheless a strong student and an excellent athlete. Good-looking but not handsome, he was polite without being ingratiating—"southern charm," John called it, giving no derogatory twist to the phrase. Among John's colleagues, Chase was known as the kind of boy who had a bright future. "He'll go places," they agreed.

As John had chatted with Chase, however, he thought he caught a whiff of alcohol on Chase's breath—a clear taboo at this school, which had a strict honor code and a firm two-strikes-and-you're-out policy against drinking on campus. John knew the policy well, and as the school's chief disciplinarian, he kept a mental tally of the handful of kids who, any given semester, already had strike one. Chase wasn't on that list, which was a good thing. On this campus, "out" literally meant expulsion for the remainder of the year—an inalterably firm stand that John had seen invoked more than once, usually resulting in a boy's leaving, never to return.

Grilled about the alcohol, Chase finally confessed that his date had brought a flask with her and that he'd taken a drink. With some regret but without a moment's hesitation, John sent them both home early from the dance. But he took no further action that night. This being a first offense, whatever needed to be sorted out with Chase's parents could wait until the following week.

Playing by the Rules

Now, however, it was Monday, and John had to explain the situation to Chase's mother, Tally. Reaching her by phone, he laid out the long history of the school's honor code and explained how the nondrinking policy fit into that framework. He also noted the two-strikes provision, making it clear that although Chase was on notice, he wasn't about to get kicked out.

To his great relief, Tally wasn't angry or defensive. She was instead apologetic, grateful, and friendly—so friendly, in fact, that she began recounting a recent conversation in which Chase had volunteered that some weeks before the prom, a friend had hidden a bottle of bourbon in his school locker and given him a drink.

The moment she began that story, John told me, his heart sank. He knew where it was headed. *Why is she telling me this?!* he said to himself. *I don't want to know!* Without that knowledge, the dance event was strike one. Now, all at once, it was strike two—and the punishment was explicit. Under the school's rules, it suddenly appeared that a fine young man with an exemplary college-bound future would have to be expelled.

To give himself time to think, John thanked Tally for her frankness and let her know he'd get back in touch with her.

In this many-layered story, there are two key players: John, the administrator, and Tally, the parent. We'll get to Tally in a minute. First, though, a word about John. He could see in this situation a right-versus-right dilemma—right to follow the rule, but also right to let Chase remain in school. What was he to do? His situation pitted truth against loyalty—and justice against mercy. On the one hand, he had every reason to come down hard on Chase. The glaring truth was that this was indeed a second offense for a boy who, while he hadn't been the instigator, had on both occasions been a willing coconspirator. Was a trend developing here that John, as a matter of justice and responsibility, needed to squelch firmly and dramatically?

On the other hand, John had learned of this earlier lapse only because of Tally's candor. What kind of signal would it send to the other parents when it became known (as it surely would) that the reward for her honesty had been a devastating penalty that could significantly affect her son's future? With Tally as a precedent, would any parent ever again speak up to the administration about things that most mattered? Would parents fear retribution when-ever they sought assistance? Didn't John owe her some loyalty, some appreciation for her helpfulness? Wasn't this a case requiring mercy, where a punishment was needed that better fit the circumstances?

The Role of Honor Codes

John's problem was that he was caught in the vice grip of a set of regulations that left him little room for creativity and might well have invited him to cry out for supernal intervention. Like King Darius in the Old Testament account of Daniel and the lions' den, John felt like a good king trapped in bad policy. Daniel, we're told, served as prime minister to Darius—to the envy of the other court-iers, who inveigled the king to sign an inalterable decree punishing anyone found worshiping anything other than Darius himself. When Daniel put his religion first and continued his daily worship, he was reported. The king worked every way he could to save his friend, only to be forced by his own policy to throw him to the lions. As it unfolds, of course, the story exemplifies courage, divine action, and just deserts—the lions shut their mouths, Daniel is rescued, and his accusers are thrown in instead. *Yes,* John thought, *bad policy. But surely there's a remedy here short of deific visitation?*

The problem, he could see, lay in the way the school defined the word *out.* Did *out* have to mean expulsion? Or should the policy have said, "Two strikes, and you will be subject to a punishment that is swift, sure, and far more severe than you had expected." Granted, that's a less catchy phrase than the original, which is borrowed from baseball's three-strike rule. The problem is that in the borrowing, the phrase ran afoul of its own metaphor. All *out* means in baseball is that you retire from the plate, to come back again later. The school had turned *out* into a terminal, life-changing condition—perhaps without ever giving the word all the thought it deserved.

Yet there are admirable schools and colleges, among them Virginia Military Institute in Lexington, Virginia, that hold an even firmer single-sanction standard. VMI asserts that for those found guilty of an honor code violation, "there is only one penalty—dismissal from the Institute."[2] Such schools, pointing to a record of exemplary obedience, argue that an unremitting focus on an honor code, and an unyielding insistence on enforcing its penalties, creates a culture of nearly universal adherence that students sign up to in advance and follow willingly and rigorously.

Rutgers University professor Donald McCabe, whose three surveys on honor codes between 1990 and 2006 established the bedrock analysis in this field, finds it increasingly hard to compare recent data with his earlier findings—in part because students today may have absorbed cheating so fully into their mind-sets that they have a hard time identifying "what truly constitutes cheating." He still, however, sees two reasons to support honor codes. Students who cheat at a school with a strong honor code, he says, "can't avoid a dialogue about whether cheating is appropriate or not." As a result, they face a decision each time they're tempted to cheat—"an exercise that may come back and help them make better decisions in the 'real' world," says McCabe. While his data show only a little less cheating at honor code schools compared to no-code institutions, the real numbers may actually be further apart. The willingness of students to lie on a survey about whether they've cheated—to say no when they've actually cheated—may mean that the numbers for honor code schools are, he says, "more accurate than at no-code schools," creating a greater differential in favor of honor-code schools. Noting that "obviously I can't state that with any real proof," McCabe says he is still willing to "stand behind honor codes as a preferred strategy" for reducing cheating.[3]

But shouldn't any good policy offer well-meaning administrators room for flexibility? In the realm of ethics, isn't each case bound to be somewhat different? Could a regimen that says there is "only one penalty—dismissal" actually be fair? As John contemplated Chase's case, those kinds of questions kept arising. He could see that justice properly needs to set up expectations about behaviors. It needs to invoke sanctions for infractions that are clear, firm, and evenly applied. But shouldn't it also consider exceptions? And wasn't Chase's story just that kind of demand for mercy? Wasn't the school's policy mired in a right-versus-wrong view of ethics and oblivious to the tough choice facing a school administrator struggling with a right-versus-right dilemma?

And yet (as the proponents of honor codes might argue) the arguments for making an exception arose only because the code was not sufficiently reinforced, publicized, and held in awe. Had it been so, wouldn't Tally's own antennae have gone up the moment Chase told her about the locker incident? Wouldn't she have in effect become an extension of the school's own enforcement system, condemning Chase's behavior and warning him of grave consequences if he and his friends didn't instantly stop this behavior? Might not Chase, in that context, have firmly refused his date's offer of the flask—and perhaps even rebuked her for potentially endangering the careers of other boys at the school? Might the supporters of a stern honor code have used Chase's case to make their point: that such a code requires persistent reminders to the students of the dangers of disobedience? Wouldn't they argue that the worst combination is a tough honor code, descending fiercely on every infraction, coupled with a weak communications program that creates a culture of casual disregard for the rules?

John clearly has a challenge. But so does Tally. As the parent in this situation, what is she to do? It might seem that the solution is out of her hands and beyond her scope—and that her choices are either to await a dreaded outcome that she herself inadvertently prompted or raise a blistering attack on the school in defense of her boy. In fact, there's a third way out—a trilemma option—that parents sometimes overlook: the power of a well-reasoned, clear-headed moral argument.

The word *moral* is key here. If all Tally has to offer is a *legal* argument, she'll find herself talking not with the school's administrators but with its legal counsel. If, in defense, she wraps herself in her own lawyers, she may end with a Pyrrhic victory so poisonous to the atmosphere that Chase, though allowed to remain, would become an unwelcome guest at his own school. So suppose that instead, Tally goes the *political* route: she lines up powerful parents and trustees on her side in an effort to neutralize John or even remove him from his post. Again, she may win, but at the cost of lasting animosity among those who support a firm no-drinking policy. Finally, what if she goes for an *economic* approach? If she threatens to withhold financial contributions and urges others to do the same, she's always at risk of encountering pockets deeper than her own among those who, aligned with the administration, could make her fight a futile one.

A moral argument, instead, takes the issues back to the root question, which is not, "Who wins?" but, "What's right?" Appealing to the deepest motivations of the entire community, such an argument positions her as lifting the conversation away from polarizing assertions about right versus wrong and into the realm of right versus right. In this realm, she'll find no need to develop arguments proving that one side or the other has malicious intent, incompetent execution, or illogical rationality. Nor will she need to resort to ad hominem attacks against the character of others. She can instead keep the discussion on the level of concepts and principles rather than people and personalities. Recognizing that what makes the entire issue difficult is the right-versus-right nature of the debate, she won't be tempted to address it using a merely right-versus-wrong methodology, but will be able to ground it in values-based reasoning at every turn.

But can Tally—or any other mother without a doctorate in moral philosophy—do that? Of course she can. For fourteen years she's been having exactly this conversation, a little bit at a time, with Chase. How do we know? First, her initial response to John was immediately receptive to the school's firm stand on ethical issues, suggesting that she was no stranger to the "What's right?" question. And second, the fact that Chase confided in her about the earlier drinking episode tells us reams about their relationship. He may have anticipated a rebuke from her—aimed principally at the student who brought in the bourbon, but landing squarely on himself as well. But he also expected a conversation driven by logic and friendliness rather than emotion and accusation. In many families, sadly, the default position would be for the teenager never to share such a story with a parent. Things were apparently different in this family, and that difference has readied Tally for this larger conversation with John about social drinking, school policy, and Chase's future.

Not Going It Alone

As she prepares for this conversation with John, Tally needs to take one cardinal rule of ethical decision making to heart: don't go it alone. Ethics isn't for loners, but for those of us who live in communities. Not surprisingly, our best decisions don't happen on isolated mountaintops or solo kayak rides. They happen in the company of others. Most parents have, or can pull together, a few people to help them think through such questions. Some may live next door, while others may be across the country. Some may be reachable over coffee the next morning, while others may be at the end of an e-mail. Some may be family members, while others may be friends and acquaintances. Some may be education professionals, while others may be interested nonspecialists. They may represent an array of ages and perspectives. Whoever they are, the most helpful ones will each have a caring relationship to Tally, education, and ethics. The resulting dialogue will be as rich, nuanced, and clarifying as Tally wants to make it.

I have no record of how Tally actually sorted through this question. But let me share with you how we did. When we published a version of John's dilemma on June 26, 2007, in our weekly newsletter, *Ethics Newsline*, we invited readers to respond. The comments, in e-mails from across the United States and Canada, suggest something of what Tally might have found had she asked for help.

First, what might she have learned from professional educators in the independent school network? "John's dilemma is more complicated than it appears on the surface," writes Patrick F. Bassett, president of the National Association of Independent Schools.

> Many independent schools have a variation on the disciplinary theme: some are one-strike schools, most are two-strike schools, and some are three-strike (or more) schools, all related to school mission, culture, climate and values.
>
> Using the Institute for Global Ethics' own rubric, independent schools consider caring (mercy) versus universal principles (justice) on a daily basis. But the policy, especially for the one- or two-strike schools, recognizes that while adolescents make mistakes (as do adults), there are some mistakes that we cannot tolerate (selling drugs on campus, for example) because they run counter to the larger values (self-discipline) and needs (attracting families who share our values) of the school community.

Schools with tougher and more consistent sanctions believe two things:

1. The certainty of a severe punishment prevents "crime" and allows potential "fellow travelers" to use an excuse that is acceptable in the peer culture: "Can't do that, since my parents would kill me if I got kicked out!"

2. Parental reaction ("How could you do this to my child, who has had such a good record to this point?") and student reaction ("The school authorities just don't get the pressure we are under"), while genuinely emotional, are unrelated to the higher purpose of the system, which is: to send strong signals about community expectations and guide behavior in strong and unequivocal ways.

John's dilemma would be solved in most cases by the administrator recognizing that hearsay doesn't count in these high-stakes situations; only the direct evidence discovered by school authorities is relevant.

Seeking further counsel, Tally might have those comments reaffirmed by another independent school educator. "I think it ought to be understood," writes Jon Rosenshine, director of the upper school at the Buckley School in New York City, "that strike two cannot follow retroactively after strike one."

In other words, there first has to be a strike one with consequences, discussion, and support for the student. Only then, after the student has had a chance to internalize the situation and potentially learn from it, can he or she be held responsible for a second strike.

But even with this adjustment, I agree that no policy should ever be so hard and fast that you are bound to choose to follow the procedure of the rule to the detriment of the substantive purpose of the disciplinary process. Any discussion of disciplinary issues ought to recognize the interplay between procedure and sub-stance. Absolute consistency necessarily leads to unfair-ness anyway, as students and their situations are rarely consistent. While this leaves an administration open to some calls of unfairness and inconsistency, that is a battle worth fighting in order to avoid having to inflict an unsuitable punishment.

So I would handle the parent's admission as a supple-mentary issue in the first strike; then I would deal with the locker incident and the prom incident together because they are coming to our attention at the same time. I would also make it very clear to the mom that the repercussions of strike one are not significantly worse as a result of what she told the school; otherwise, it would be a huge mistake to betray her trust. A disciplinary consequence will follow a discussion of these matters as well as some form of treatment or counseling, and a second strike could happen only following this process.

As though summarizing these points, Tally might then hear from someone like Professor David Kaiser of Hamline University in Saint Paul, Minnesota, who writes, "John should remember that policies are intended to serve a higher purpose, e.g. mission, vision, and values. If life were mechanical and robotic, simply following policies would do, and administrators could be replaced by robots. Life, however, is complex and dynamic, and decision-making is a humane undertaking. John should decide in accordance with the higher intentions of the institution and its constituents—and he should rewrite the policy to ensure that it is human and humane, not mechanistic and robotic."

Along with educators, however, Tally will also hear from parents themselves—forcefully, perhaps, and on both sides of the issue. Some, like Michael Deming from West Gardiner, Maine, will be strong supporters of following the rigor of the policy.

"John has two events," he writes, "that show a definite trend of either going along with the crowd or of a potentially serious alcohol addiction. Both events happened when Chase thought no one was looking. One event could be a fluky happenstance, but two is the conception of a trend, and a trend gives birth to a way of life.

"So there is no ethical dilemma. The policy was not intended to be punitive, but to keep these kinds of events from being subtly 'winked at' and latently approved of. A thoughtful leader teaches that in real life, behavior has its results, whether for good or ill. There are no exceptions. A wise mother once told me that 'we often hold people back by holding them up.'"

Tally may also hear from the likes of Donovan Jacobs of Encino, California:

> If you follow the "logic" of the two strikes rule, a kid with an exemplary record gets thrown out of school because he's been discovered to be drinking twice, though he hasn't actually been caught doing it in one case, and hasn't done anything while drinking either time to warrant any other penalties. Meanwhile, a kid who gets drunk out of his mind and wraps his car around a telephone pole presumably suffers no penalty for alcohol use because it only happened once.
>
> This is only slightly stupider than the "zero tolerance" policies so popular in other schools. Yes, the policy teaches that actions have consequences, but in such a heavy-handed way that the only rule that *really* gets taught to its victims and witnesses is: Don't Get Caught.

Tally will also pick up some quieter language that provides her with additional arguments. "When an arbitrary rule backs someone in authority into a corner," writes T. J. Marton of Erie, Pennsylvania, "it's time to question the value of the rule itself. Judgment, mercy, intelligence, and empathy are essential components of treating people fairly." She might, in fact, even want to quote Seth Phillips of Quesnel, British Columbia, Canada, who writes that "morally, the policy would seem excessively harsh and somewhat arbitrary. It's probable that most such 'first-strike' incidents are not caught—and thus bad luck or lack of slyness would be the most likely precursor to punishment."

Using the Five Core Values to Make Your Case

By engaging in conversations of this sort with a few close friends and family members, and perhaps seeking advice from some experienced educators, Tally will begin to formulate an ethical position on this issue. Judging from the comments we received, she would be on solid moral ground to argue, on the basis of her core values, that

1. *Fairness* dictates that the locker incident not be considered a first strike, since it never provided any opportunity for warning, counsel, and reform prior to the second strike.

2. *Responsibility* requires that policies for expulsion need to be so vigorously communicated and discussed with students that there's little chance that they'll be overlooked or ignored.

3. *Honesty* demands that parents be encouraged to speak freely and confidentially, with no fear that their words will be used against them or their child.

4. *Respect* insists that although tough, consistent policies are essential, the cases they cover involve the dignity and humanity of individuals, where the interplay between justice and mercy can never be automatically determined.

5. *Compassion* suggests that the caring support of those who misbehave, coupled with firm efforts at correction and reform, will send a powerful signal that the school values each student.

But will it matter? Would Tally be heard if she asked for a meeting with John to discuss these points? Or is the whole system so rigid that there's no wiggle room and no use protesting? "Truth be known," continues Pat Bassett in his e-mail response, after decades of watching how schools actually discipline students, "even one-strike schools build some 'air in the system,' individually and subjectively, for just such situations." And if the school remains unbending? "Kids who do get expelled," Bassett concludes, "often report back that it was a salubrious, life-changing event, not the 'end-of-life-as-we-know-it' event it seemed at the time. I can't tell you how many schools have alumni trustees who were once expelled from the school and have later returned as patrons, leaders, and parents who send their own children to the school."

For Tally, then, the challenge is to discover and articulate those moral points that help the administrators see more clearly the essential arguments of this situation. For John, the challenge is to uphold the justice of the policy while invoking the compassion required by the circumstances. Neither has an easy road. But if all that either knows about ethics is that it's about right versus wrong, neither will be successful in finding the middle ground that this dilemma so powerfully demands.

Lessons from   Zero Tolerance

- A strict honor code can be a powerful incentive for right-doing—or a bad policy that traps good people. If your child's school has a code, be sure it makes sense—and be willing to speak up if it doesn't.
- The test of a good parent-child relationship is candid communication, where kids tell you when they've done wrong. Don't allow that candor to be penalized.
- Good school cultures teach students to obey their core values. Bad ones teach kids to be sly and try never to get caught.
- When parents must defend their children, their best ally is often a moral, not a legal, argument. Values clearly expressed keep you on the ethical high ground.

Avoiding Bystander Apathy

As a parent, Tally had no choice but to be involved in Chase's moral development. But what if you're not the parent, but simply a witness to an ethical challenge?

That's where Terri found herself early in June, when she arrived back for a new season at the summer camp she was part of. As a longtime trustee, she once again had volunteered to help the counselors open up the cabins for the children who, by month's end, would pour into this northern Maine lakeside facility.

That week, an environmental education program had rented the camp. The program supplied its own instructors to work with a group of sixth graders from a local middle school. She'd always felt comfortable with kids that age, she told me. But neither Terri nor her camp counselors had any official role with their program, so she hardly could have suspected that one of these kids would open for her a moral can of worms that, months later, still troubled her.

Like so many other moral issues, this one unfolded almost instantaneously and caught Terri wholly by surprise. She was sitting by the water's edge after dinner, enjoying the fading summer evening with several counselors, when a group of kids from the environmental program came down to fish. Their instructors led them to various rocks along the shore where they could cast their bobbers into the still water. One child, Terri noted, had brought an elaborate tackle box, out of which he took a paper cup of worms.

"You can't use those," an instructor told him.

"Why not?" he asked.

Because, the instructor explained, this lake has stringent envi-ronmental standards: motorboats aren't permitted, and no live bait is allowed.

Unfazed, the child went right on baiting his hook. "Nobody will know," he replied, noting that there weren't any wardens around to catch him.

The instructor simply shrugged, said nothing, and walked away. The boy cast his worm into the lake.

What should Terri have done?

On the one hand, she recalls, "it bothered me, sitting there, that here was a teachable moment that was lost" due to the instructor's indifference. What a great opportunity, she felt, to make a point about law, obedience, responsibility, respect, fairness—any one of a host of virtues. Would the boy have been responsive? He was, she felt, "just a normal kid in jeans and a T-shirt, not a hoodlum." What's more, there were three adult instructors with the environmental program who, she said, "had been doing this for fifteen or twenty years." Surely, she felt, it was their responsibility to train these children to obey environmental regulations.

On the other hand, would it have been right for her to intervene, countermand the instructor's indifference, and help the boy grasp these things? She had no role in that week's program, so would she have been seen simply as a meddling adult inserting herself where she didn't belong? Besides, though she'd been visiting that lake for years, she wasn't an angler herself, so she'd never known about the no-worms rule. Only later did she learn that the local lake association, concerned about introducing alien species into the waters, had recently banned any use of live bait.

In the end, the moment passed, and Terri did nothing. Yet the more she thought about it afterward, the more disappointed she grew with her own inaction. Had Terri known the no-worms rule and been alone with the boy when he baited his hook, would she have spoken up? No doubt. Did she fail to act out of uncertainty, or because of the presence of others, or through a combination of both? Who knows? What she's sure about is the problem she witnessed: "the lack of respect of kids for their teachers," as she put it, "and of teachers for the kids." So despite her clarity, had she been sucked into a phenomenon known as bystander apathy? A term often used in connection with the 1964 murder of Kitty Genovese, whose cries for help went unheeded by numerous neighbors in Queens, New York, it describes the apparent paralysis that overtakes those who could offer help but who, because they are only bystanders and because others are also watching, fail to act. Although there is little to link a horrific murder in Queens with a can of worms in Maine, that concept, as researchers explain, also describes inhibitions in situations far less serious than capital crimes—where, in the presence of an audience of others who also fail to act, it becomes easier to justify your own inactivity and dilute your sense of responsibility.

Should You Intervene? Four Questions to Help You Decide

That dilution of responsibility—especially in situations where, as a parent, you see other people's children engaged in wrongdoing— regularly raises wrenching choices for parents who care about ethics. Certainly you long to see parents nurturing a clear moral flame in their own children. When that's not there, what can you do—and, more important, what *should* you do? What is the morally right approach—the defining *ought* in this situation—that tells you how to respond? How can Terri—as a nonparent, bystander, and chance observer, on one hand, but as a trustee, ethical champion, and experienced parent, on the other—think this through?

Four questions may help here:

———————

1. *What's the real issue?* Even a simple narrative, like Terri's can-of-worms story, can have complex ethical layerings. Is this about fishing regulations (no live bait), or willful disobedience ("Nobody will know"), or disrespect (by the child), or irresponsibility (by the counselor)? This particular chain of events began with the regulations. Had there been no prohibition of live bait, there would have been nothing unethical for Terri to notice. But the moral question facing Terri has less to do with bait than with values. What if the use of live bait were okay on this lake? And

what if Terri still witnessed a similar pattern of student disrespect and adult indifference? She would still have had plenty of reason to be upset and want to intervene. Suppose, however, that bait were prohibited but that the counselor had immediately sought to address and correct the child's disrespect. Would Terri have then been upset? Probably not. She would have seen a problem being corrected the moment it arose. The point at issue here, then, is not about rules but values. That's why Terri, even without knowing the no-live-bait rule, immediately reacted to this situation and wrestled with her proper role.

2. *Which of these values is most important?* There are at least three antivalues in play in this story: disrespect, irresponsibility, and unfairness. Terri's immediate instinct is to address the disrespect by confronting the student. But isn't the real culprit here the irresponsibility of the counselor? Suppose she had a choice. Suppose she could magically correct the child so strongly that he would never again disrespect adult authority. Or suppose she could so masterfully reform the counselor that he would forever afterward take proactive steps to correct errant children. Obviously the latter course of action—encouraging a counselor who might have occasion to intervene with hundreds of children each year—carries a far larger potential payoff than simply adjusting one child's behavior.

3. *But what about the unfairness?* What should her response be to the all-too-common student habit of trying to get away with something, keep things hidden, and prosper through invisible cheating? If all she wanted to address were the child's disrespect, she could have done so without ever mentioning his "nobody will know" justification. She doesn't need to refute his argument to let him know, in no uncertain terms, that deliberate disregard for a teacher is wrong. If, however, she can also find ways to correct not just his behavior but his fundamental view of the world, which would have the greater impact? The answer, clearly, is the latter. Of course, it's easier to bark out, "Shape up, and obey!" than to

ask, "Why do you think it's okay to do whatever you want so long as you don't get caught?" But if, as you correct the behavior, you carry the discussion far enough to expose the child's fundamental misconception about right and wrong, he may have to rethink his notion that the only wrong thing is getting caught. Such a discussion probably entails a conversation about the kind of world that student wants to live in. If everyone around him sets out deliberately to cheat—and to hide that fact—is that the finest world he can imagine? What if, every time he caught a fish, it were taken away from him by a warden—who, it turns out, was only someone dressed as a warden, but who regularly stole fish from anglers because "nobody will know"? Isn't it clear that those who live by cheating always risk being outcheated by others?

4. *What's the hardest course of action for Terri?* It's probably tougher to confront the counselor than discipline the child. If she does settle for addressing the child, however, the easier and less courageous way lies in simply demanding compliance. The harder course will be to dismantle one of the child's defining clichés. In other words, there is a range of morally courageous options in this narrative. Terri may have assumed this road had only one fork: she either expresses moral courage or she doesn't. In fact, there are several ways forward. The simplest would be to holler through the woods, "Hey, kid, stop using worms!"—a course that might prove surprisingly effective. At the other extreme, she could seek to convene all the counselors, kids, and camp staff to discuss this question in detail. In between, she could run after the counselor right then, or quietly approach the counselor later, or approach the counselor's superiors, or approach her own camp's management team.

It is little wonder, then, that Terri found herself baffled—and, to some extent, paralyzed. The situation confronting her held an array of choices. But when we break it open and examine its inner workings, the various pressure points and possibilities for action come into view. We can then apply straightforward moral reasoning to determine the best way forward. The point for Terri—and for any other adult caught in a nonparenting ethical conundrum—is threefold:

- Recognize that the seemingly simple narrative thread facing you may be woven of several distinct ethical strands—and be willing to do the untangling.

- When the threads are separated, choose which to follow. It may be the one with the largest potential for good. Or it may be the one you can most easily follow at the moment, given the resources of time and energy available. Or it may be the one most familiar to you, because you've followed something like it before. Whichever it is, make a choice and commit to a course of action.

- Don't allow the argument of complexity to paralyze your purpose. True, at her picnic table that evening, Terri may not have had time to pursue all the arguments I've laid out here. But remember that we're building ethical fitness—creating reserves of intuitional strength and ability you can call on when these sudden moments arise. Go back and revisit ethical situations once they've passed—as Terri certainly did. Then trust the process, and you'll find that every encounter with a nonparental ethical conundrum will make you stronger and more intuitively adept at responding.

Why Taking a Stand for Conscience Helps Nations as Well as Children

What will make the difference next time for Terri? The answer lies in two words: moral courage. It's not that Terri lacked core values. Quite the opposite: those values were so salient in her mind that immediately, right there along the shore that evening, she saw disrespect for adult authority and irresponsibility by the instructor, along with a sense of self-seeking unfairness and duplicity evidenced in the "nobody will know" argument. Nor was she lacking in moral reasoning. The importance of rules in general, the arguments for this particular no-worms rule, the specious nature of the "nobody will know" excuse, and the moral anarchy implied in the refusal of the instructor to assert his authority—these all stood out to her in unambiguous clarity. What was missing was the courage to take action when her values-based reasoning was put to the test—the courage to move from conscience to accomplishment, from insight to performance, from knowing to doing.

Terri's experience, small though it is, has big-picture implications. In recent years, how many financial sector employees, minding their business by their own metaphorical lakesides, suddenly observed corporate corruption, deception, and deliberate rule breaking? How many of the rule breakers were, in effect, moral adolescents—fully mature adults, of course, but with no more conscience than that kid with the tackle box and with no justification more sophisticated than, "Nobody will know, so it's okay"? How many of these bystanders said and did nothing? And how many now are sensing, in the ethical collapses that swept the economy into a grinding recession, the fruits of their silent inaction?

I'll have more to say about moral courage in the next chapter. But one thing is sure: people can be taught moral courage. It's better to do it at the bank of a lake, however, than a bank on Wall Street—and better to catch them early, some summer evening by the shore, when they think nobody's watching. Either way, however, that teaching won't happen unless the adults in children's lives—parents and nonparents alike—recognize the need, set the standard, and enforce the moral positions. When adults set the bar low, as Terri told me, kids aim low, but "when you hold the standard up to kids, they'll hit it."

Next time, she says, "I'm going to step up."

Avoiding Bystander Apathy

- Facing moral dilemmas when you're not the parent is sometimes harder than when you are. Ask whether you're standing for conscience or just meddling.
- Probe for the real issue. Untangle the narrative until you find what's really at stake, and don't let complexity paralyze your purpose.
- Standing by to help if needed can be hugely valuable. Bystander apathy, however, can be fatal. It's better to act and be rebuffed than live with regret.
- Moral courage is contagious even though it may seem lonely at the time. The power of a single right example is enormous.

Dan and the Marijuana: Standing for Principle

When do children start standing for principle? As developmental psychologist Lawrence Kohlberg observed in the 1950s, that capacity arrives late in a child's moral development. It comes to full fruition only during what Kohlberg called the two final, or "principled," stages of his famous six stages of moral judgment.

(continued)

At the earliest, lowest level, he argued, children do right simply from fear of punishment or respect for authority. By stage 2 they learn about equal exchange and fairness, though they still believe that a rule should be followed only when it's in your own (or someone else's) immediate interest. In stage 3 they increasingly take account of others, recognize stereotypes of "good" behavior, grasp the Golden Rule, and accept such values as trust, loyalty, respect, and gratitude. By stage 4, as they see that a generalized moral system defines rules and roles, morality hinges on fulfilling agreed-upon duties.

In stage 5 (the first of Kohlberg's "principled" stages), children accept a social contract requiring obedience to shared laws and basing ethics on the greatest good for the greatest number. In the sixth and final stage, morality becomes a matter of broad universals, with children paying less attention to consequences than to principles. Here, at last, they develop personal commitments to justice, equal human rights, and individual dignity.

Or at least they do in theory. When parents actually see their children behaving this way—when they see them suddenly express moral courage out of conviction rather than stubbornness or chutzpah—the result can be surprising, encouraging, and sometimes complicated, as Al learned the day the school called.

"My son Dan, in seventh grade, was one of three or four students suspected of having marijuana," Al wrote me. "They were going to search their lockers and their pockets. My son refused to permit them to search his person, so they called me."

When Al arrived at school, the administrators were asking Dan to turn out his pockets. "It's not like it's a strip search," the principal said.

"I looked at Dan. I could see he was determined.

"'Do you have any marijuana in your pockets, Dan?'" I asked him.

" 'No.' "

" 'Then why not just turn them out?' "

" 'It's the principle. They told me I had to, and that's a forced search.' "

"I was stumped. I stumbled around a bit, finally agreeing that I would not tell him to empty out his pockets if he felt that strongly about it. Turning to the principal, I said something like, 'I'm sorry, but I'm not going to force him to do something he feels strongly about.' "

"Then I added, 'Maybe if you just asked him nicely . . .' "

"The principal said, 'Dan, would you please empty your pockets?' "

"Dan smiled and said, 'Sure.' "

"There was no marijuana."

A simple tale, it reminds parents to be on the lookout for four important surprises:

- *Children learn things in school.* Studying the Bill of Rights, Dan had heard about freedom from unwarranted search and seizure. Not surprisingly, he found a personal application for that concept.
- *Children translate abstract concepts into moral imperatives.* We know kids test limits, so why be surprised when they test principles? Dan's real question was, "Are principles just theoretical, or do they work in a grown-up world?"
- *Children learn moral courage earlier than we think.* Dan put himself at risk for his values. Don't be surprised when conscience suddenly emerges, and be sure to honor it.
- *Parents are sometimes stumped.* Don't be surprised when you don't always see the answer right away. Nobody does, so cut yourself some slack. Trust your intuitions, and take the path that honors the highest principle—in this case, the conviction that Dan was a good kid making a tough choice.

Showing Moral Courage

When June's fourteen-year-old son, Trevor, returned to school in the fall, he seemed happy enough. But she soon began hearing about Brian, the new kid in the class. Burly, surly, and belligerent, he had singled out Trevor as the target of his bullying. As the days mounted up, so did the abuse, ratcheting up from nasty innuendo through explicit threat and finally on to pushing, shoving, and tripping. June was pretty sure that Trevor was keeping his cool and not responding in kind. But she could tell he was deeply troubled.

The problem had not gone unnoticed by teachers and administrators. But this school had never been quick to expel problem students, choosing instead to work with them wherever possible. Brian's parents knew about the problem, and they discussed it with Brian. After these discussions, the bullying would seem to abate for a while, only to flare up again without warning. Nothing seemed to break the cycle.

As June talked with the administrators, she could see them searching for a solution that would keep Brian in school. She agreed that they shouldn't throw him out. That would only hand the problem along to some other school, and where was the fairness in that? She could see, too, that while they had tried various avenues, there was one they hadn't pursued: having Trevor talk directly to Brian and ask him to knock it off.

"No way!" said Trevor, when June first raised that option across the kitchen table one evening. "He'll think I'm a wimp, and it'll make the situation even worse."

As June pursued the conversation, she began to talk about moral courage. Yes, it would take guts to stand up to Brian. But nothing else was getting through to him. Maybe he needed to hear from a peer rather than an adult. Brian would no doubt respect a stand based on physical courage. If Trevor were bigger than Brian, stood his ground, and pushed back, the bully would certainly back down. Was there a chance that a similarly firm stand based on *moral* courage would change things?

Understanding the Three Elements of Moral Courage

Moral courage can be defined as the willing endurance of significant danger for the sake of principle. It's characterized by real and recognized risk. It requires a willingness to endure that risk—to take a stand in the face of danger. And it happens because some overarching matters of conscience—values, virtues, principles— are at stake. Put graphically, it looks like the diagram in Figure 4.1.

Take away the "values" circle at the top, and you're left with what we all know as physical courage—a hugely important quality, but one that, without the values component, is just as useful to a Mafia hit man as to a teenage bungee jumper. Remove the "danger" circle, and you're left with either a situation having no risk at all—which takes no courage to withstand—or a case where the dangers are unrecognized, and your willingness to endure them may simply be naive, if not downright dumb. Finally, take away the "endurance" circle, and you end up with strong values but a danger so threatening that you bolt as fast as you can—a condition usually called *cowardice*. Put the three circles together, and you've got real moral courage—which, at its simplest, is the

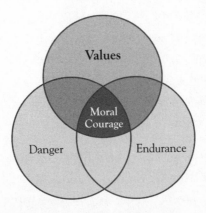

Figure 4.1 The Elements of Moral Courage

courage (the two bottom circles) to be moral (the top circle). If *being moral* means living by your core values, then moral courage consists of taking action when your values are put to the test.

June knew that Trevor felt strongly about his values, particularly about fairness, respect, and responsibility. He had always insisted that it was wrong to take unfair advantage of people. He wasn't tempted to disrespect someone just because that person disrespected him. And he was generally willing to shoulder responsibility, even when the circumstances were not of his own making. So should he, at this point, have the courage to put those values into action?

An adult might say, "Of course—it's no big deal." But what looks like a low-risk gambit to a parent may seem to be an enormous challenge to an adolescent. The obvious dangers ranged all the way from an unpleasant conversation to an intensification of the bullying—including, perhaps, a public mockery of his motives that could brand him as a sissy and make him the laughingstock of the school.

In addition, lurking around the edges of every situation where moral courage is required are three more subtle fears—any of which, according to our research, can be a powerful invisible inhibitor to moral courage:

1. *Fear of ambiguity*, where we fail to act because we don't think we know everything we need to know

2. *Fear of individual loss*, where we dread the disappearance of career, job, wealth, reputation, or some other solid or intangible personal asset

3. *Fear of public exposure*, where we shrink from taking the lead, getting out front, or becoming a target

For Trevor, this situation held little ambiguity: Brian's intentions were clear. Nor did he stand to lose his stuff, his friends, or his good nature. The real fear here had to do with public exposure: *Why me? How come I have to be the point man?*

As he and his mother talked it through that evening, she knew that she herself had to embody the qualities she wanted him to express. She needed to be fair—to be sure she wasn't putting an unfair burden on her son. She had to show respect for his intuitions and be willing to back away if he didn't feel right about it. Yet in her role as responsible parent, she knew something had to be done. It would be irresponsible to blow off the Brian problem and hope it would just go away. But she also needed to be sure she wasn't using her authority to manipulate, pressure, or wheedle her son into a course of action that could make the situation worse. She knew it had to be his decision.

In the end, Trevor reluctantly agreed. The school authorities asked the boys to meet in the school office, with the principal as the only adult present. Trevor explained how the bullying made him feel, and he asked Brian to stop. Not surprisingly, Brian burst forth with a predictable litany of excuses—denying that he had been a bully, then explaining that it was all a joke, then taking offense that he was being accused. Trevor quietly persisted until, a few minutes into the conversation, Brian suddenly broke down in tears. Pouring out his own story of abuse and victimization at his previous school, he admitted he wanted to be friends with other kids but that he didn't know how. And he promised to change his behavior.

In the weeks that followed, June remembers, Brian tried hard to keep his word. And while the issue wasn't completely resolved, she knew her son had made the right decision when, a few months later, she was helping him organize a skating party. Brian's name was on the list of Trevor's invitees.

If you think moral courage is something that gets expressed only by people like Joan of Arc, Winston Churchill, or Nelson Mandela, you might not even use that term to describe Trevor's experience. But moral courage is not some saintly behavior reserved for a few noble figures at moments of calamity. It's a bread-and-butter issue at work within our daily lives. There are times when we need it to get up in the morning just to go to work—or to cut short a midnight conversation so we can be rested for tomorrow. It's what gives us the guts to make the unpleasant phone call, address that lingering problem with the boss, confront the neighbor who won't pick up after his dog, or begin the morning commute. It allows parents to face up to stark issues they'd rather not address with children, from drugs and sex to deception and apathy. Far more frequently, however, it shapes the contours of our day by urging us to make the unpleasant but necessary decisions, address little habits before they become defining characteristics, and get into conversations with our kids that they may not want to have. But most often, in well-balanced families, it flows out naturally as we encourage our children to stand for conscience over convenience and promise keeping over self-gratification.

Parents Can Be Catalysts Even When They're Not Decision Makers

As is so often the case in parenting, June's role was that of a catalyst. She wasn't required to express moral courage herself. Had she tried to meet with Brian, in fact, she might well have derailed the process of reconciliation. She had to do something harder: work patiently and quietly with Trevor along three lines:

- *Listen carefully, recognize the situation, and offer her support.* Some parents might have dismissed Brian's bullying as a kids-will-be-kids issue. Others might have told Trevor to learn kickboxing or karate, teaching him to fight physical violence with physical courage. Still others might have forced the principal to move Trevor out of that class—or even pulled him out of that school and sent him to another. Instead, June saw this situation as an opportunity to express moral courage.

- *Reason it through until the right plan occurs.* Notice
  that June's strategy didn't come to her in solitude,
  and it didn't come instantly. Setting the right course
  for ethical action comes as often through conversations
  with other adults and family members as during solitary
  walks on a lonely beach. And it almost always comes
  in the wake of an engaged discussion, not as a bolt of
  inspiration the instant the problem appears.

- *Engage in mentoring without manipulating.* There's a
  happy medium between inertia and overkill. The best
  ethical coaching, advising, and mentoring focuses less
  on what someone should do than on how he or she
  thinks about doing it. Reasoning the situation through
  with Trevor, June was able to help him see that
  something had to break the logjam, and that he just
  might be the one to do it. But while she had to be
  persistent in addressing his concerns, she had to
  be willing to back away if he refused.

In the end, June's efforts paid off, probably far better than any alternative. Had Trevor tried to exempt himself from the bully's focus—by fighting back or moving elsewhere—he would have helped only himself. Instead, Trevor helped the whole school by bringing Brian into the fold. June didn't give Trevor fighting skills or an escape route. She taught him how to express moral courage, which benefited the whole community. Along the way, he was learning some of the attributes that, as I explained in my 2005 book *Moral Courage*, typically define individuals of real moral courage:

- A greater confidence in values than in personalities

- A high tolerance for ambiguity, public exposure, and
  personal risk

- A willingness to accept deferred gratification and simple rewards

- A notable independence of thought

- A formidable persistence and determination

Perhaps most important, she was teaching him to handle fear. "Courage," quipped John Wayne, "is being scared to death, and saddling up anyway." Kids need to know that the popular T-shirt mantra, "No Fear," isn't the point. What brings them into morally courageous action—and ultimately into adulthood—is not the bravura that overlooks danger or pretends to an imperviousness, but the candid assessment of risk and the commitment to move forward in spite of it. Trevor didn't dismiss his fears; he mastered them. There's a world of difference.

Lessons from   **Showing Moral Courage**

- Moral courage is the willing endurance of significant danger for the sake of principle. Real bravery lies at the point where these three intersect.
- Moral courage can be derailed by fear of ambiguity ("Don't know enough"), public exposure ("Don't put me out front"), or private loss ("Can't risk my job").
- Courage isn't fearlessness. Where nothing's at stake, courage isn't needed—a helpful point when kids say, "I'm scared," but have to keep moving.
- Parents can be catalysts—tiny additions that create huge momentum. A few words and lots of patience can sometimes produce unexpectedly fine results.

5

Ages Fifteen Through Eighteen

As children burst into their midteens, parenting begins a subtle shift away from teaching and coaching and toward dialogue and discussion. What doesn't change, however, is parental commitment—just being there, whatever the circumstance. Given all the shifts in appearance and mannerisms kids go through at this time in their lives, parents need to be simultaneously flexible and firm. How to do that? Here an adage often attributed to Thomas Jefferson rings particularly true: In matters of style, swim with the current; in matters of principle, stand like a rock.

Barbara Coloroso, author of *Kids Are Worth It! Giving Your Child the Gift of Inner Discipline*, explains her title in similar terms:

> [Kids] are worth it *because* they are children and for no other reason. They have dignity and worth simply because they are. They don't need to prove their value as human beings; they don't have to prove their worthiness to us; nor do they need to earn our affection. Our love for them cannot be conditional, although our likes and dislikes can be. We don't have to like their hairdos, the earrings in the nose, or their strange-looking shoes. Our love for them does have to be something they can count on, something they know will always be

there, even when they are in trouble and we'd probably rather not be there. Being there when they are resting comfortably in our arms, smiling up at us for the first time, is easy; being there when they are cutting teeth, colicky, and crying through the night is not. Being there when they learn to ride a two-wheeler is easy; being there when they have wrecked the family car is not. Being there when they are performing in the school play is easy; being there when they call from the police station is not.[1]

But "being there" for the preschooler is different from "being there" for the midteen, especially in the moral realm. For the younger kids, parenting can be more implicit, declarative, and action oriented—more example than explanation. But as kids mature, the ever-present "Why?" begins to turn to questions of right and wrong. Where a seven year old is comfortable knowing that something is right, a teenager is wondering why it's right—and whether there's another way of seeing it. As the right-wrong sharpness of grammar school gives way to the nuances and complexities of the teen years, the task of moral parenting becomes more richly exploratory. That doesn't mean parenting becomes intellectualized or verbose. Quite the reverse. What kids need as they move forward aren't multilayered rationalities but clear frameworks. They don't need advice on what to do so much as coaching on how to think.

If parents miss that point, they may find themselves addressing the complexities of the teenager's world and larding them with explanations that make them seem even more difficult. That's especially true if talking is your strongpoint. The task of good parenting, by contrast, is to subject the vast, roiling tempests of the teen universe to a few simple, enabling ideas. True elegance in parenting, as in science and philosophy, lies in helping others find patterns in the inscrutable and bring order to chaos.

Finding the Third Way

So far in this book, we've been talking about ethical dilemmas as though they were essentially simple, two-sided structures. We've addressed them as though they offered dual, incompatible choices, one of which had to exclude the other. Linguistically that's fair. The word *dilemma* derives from the Greek words *di*, meaning *two*, and *lemma*, meaning *a fundamental proposition, an assumption taken for granted*. So a dilemma, by definition, has only two sides.

As children mature, however, they begin to suspect that there's more to the world than stark polarities. Facing dilemmas, they begin to ask one of the most important questions in moral philosophy: What if there's a third way? What if our best option isn't a commitment to one side or the other? What if it's a noble compromise between the two? The word *trilemma* suggests that kind of solution. It's only a metaphor, since there isn't going to be a third *lemma* involved. But the word reminds us that some of our best solutions arise when we find a third way through the problem. Such solutions happen in the middle ground, where we extract the best aspects from each side of the dilemma, discard the worst, and fashion a resolution that rises above the need for a harsh, one-side-or-the-other decision.

How Parents Can Tell a Story to Make the Point

That's how Charlie worked his way through a discussion with his eighteen-year-old daughter, Sarah, and three of her college friends during their spring break. He and his wife had rented a condo on the Carolina coast, and the students arrived in Sarah's car late one afternoon after driving ten hours from campus. When they had unpacked, Charlie's wife asked him to go for some milk. Since Sarah's car was blocking his, she flipped him her keys. As he got in, he noticed the radar detector on the dashboard.

"I don't pretend I never speed," Charlie explained. But as an individual concerned about citizenship and integrity—whose career as an educator had included teaching courses in ethics—he was bothered by radar detectors and all that they symbolized. As far as he could tell, they were the only devices sold legally, openly, and enthusiastically in the U.S. market whose sole purpose was to help you break laws. Who would buy one, he reasoned, except someone who deliberately, purposefully, and with specific forethought intended to act illegally? He was pretty sure that Sarah knew his views on that topic. He also suspected that the device belonged to one of her friends, who had forgotten to hide it away as they had piled out of the car.

What to do? He knew Sarah was smart enough to realize, once she got back into her car, that he must have spotted it. If he ignored the topic altogether, she would notice. Yet he didn't feel right crashing back into the house like Bigfoot, waving his groceries and his convictions and going on a tear about lawbreakers. What he needed was a third way out—a trilemma option that didn't pretend there was no issue at all, but that didn't trample all over their independence and get the vacation off on the wrong foot.

He thought about speaking privately to Sarah. That, at least, would satisfy his obligations as a parent. But wouldn't that be ducking his duties as a teacher? He considered discussing it politely over a meal. But wouldn't that immediately cast him as a moralizing stickler out of touch with the real world, berating them for their ethical failings as they sat staring uncomfortably at their soup? How, he wondered, could he make sure the issue came up without seeming to raise it?

At dinner that night, their lively conversation turned to social issues in the news. Like Sarah, her friends were all determined environmentalists, devoted to improving the world and disgusted by society's tolerance for ecological degradation. That's when a solution began to dawn on Charlie—a parable, he called it, though he later confessed that it "began with a wholesale fib." He described to them a news story he'd just seen (that was the fiction) about a paper mill located deep in the northern New England woods, miles from the nearest town and almost inaccessible to outsiders. For years the wastewater from the plant had been polluting a local stream, running freely through an old pipe and splashing visibly into the water. The owners had recently been ordered by state regulators to stop that outflow. Instead of shutting off the wastewater, however, they attached an electrically operated stopcock at the end of the pipe, which they connected to motion detectors mounted in nearby trees. That way, Charlie explained, whenever anyone—fishermen, hikers, state inspectors—came within range of the pipe, the valve would automatically shut off the outflow until the intruders had left, after which it would reopen and let the pollutants pour out as usual. The company had done nothing to stop the wastewater. They'd just avoided detection.

The more he got into his story, the more Sarah and her friends bridled with outrage. The very idea of evading the law in this way—ripping off the public by tricking the regulators, just so the mill owners could go on with business as usual—drove them into a frenzy of indignation. And using high-tech inventiveness for such mean-spirited ends—who would *do* such a thing?! The conversation raged on for several minutes before Sarah, glancing at her father, began to catch on.

"Wait a minute, guys!" she said. "I think he's tricking us!" After which, as Charlie recalls, they had a very good conversation about radar detectors—and about persistent and intentional lawbreaking, the artful avoidance of detection, and the ways that technological innovation can be used to mask issues that are fundamentally unethical in nature.

Like most other parents, Charlie hesitated to engage in ethical discourse with young people. Not wanting to seem old-fashioned or self-righteous, not wishing to appear naive to the realities of interstate travel and student schedules, he might have been forgiven for letting this particular conversation pass him by. Yet feeling so strongly his own standards of integrity, and yearning to help his daughter's generation toward a higher recognition of values, he might also have been excused for firmly asserting his position. As he finally worked it out, however, the conversation required no moralizing on Charlie's part—no imposition of his ethical principles on recalcitrant listeners, no preachy assertions of probity, no triumphal righteousness. Why not? Because by the time the discussion began in earnest, the values that were on the table had been put there not by Charlie but by the students themselves. It took no effort on Charlie's part to move the discussion from *is* to *ought*, from a description of a situation to a recognition of an obligation. He had simply created an analogy so apt as to be unavoidable. And with little effort on his part, he had allowed the students themselves to encounter the logical incongruities in their own moral positions involving lawbreaking, regulation, and convenience.

In a classic trilemma manner, Charlie managed to extract the best features of each side of his speak-up-or-not dilemma. While he didn't ignore the topic, he never had to raise the issue himself. And when he made the points that needed making, he found he could do it without getting typed as a Luddite reactionary or a moralizing prig.

Three Yellow Flags

Finding the trilemma option is a search very much worth undertaking. The trilemma is almost always the best-way solution, keeping emotions under control and allowing all sides to feel they've won. But this search comes with three warning flags:

- *The search isn't always easy.* Trilemma options don't usually arise at the snap of a finger. When we first encounter an ethical dilemma, we focus intensely on the two opposing sides—unpacking their complexity, analyzing their obduracy, and ascribing moral arguments in their favor. In that mind-set, we can become so focused on logical extremities and polar opposites that we pay little attention to the middle ground. But as we work through the frameworks for ethical decision making, especially in a group setting, the mind begins to reach out for the more sophisticated and elegant solutions. Trilemma options almost always arise as we're thinking hard about values, noodling through right-versus-wrong issues, and searching for the most satisfying resolution principles—in other words, as we're doing the real work of seeking to resolve tough dilemmas. That's when an imaginative flash often comes along, lighting up the mind of a participant who may have fallen silent for a moment. It's at that point that the participant reenters the conversation with a sentence that begins, "Couldn't we . . . ?" or "What if . . . ?" Notice that it took Charlie a while to formulate an effective way to address the topic. As he got into Sarah's car, his first thought was not, "Ah, I need a trilemma option!" The actual option—the parable itself—occurred to him only during the give-and-take of a dinner-table discussion.

- *Not every proposed trilemma option is a keeper.* Some are patently absurd, falling apart the moment they're uttered. Others, attractive on the surface, reveal themselves to be little more than cop-outs, appeasements, or refusals to address the core issues. Still others turn out to be subtle declarations in favor of a particular side, dressed up to look like genuinely evenhanded solutions. To find the ones that work, remember the importance of cutting through to the real dilemma at hand. Charlie's dilemma was not

about a choice between arguments for or against
radar detectors. He had no interest in a trilemma
option that blended what he saw as right with what he
knew to be wrong. For him, the wrongness of radar
detectors was a settled issue. His conundrum concerned
whether to raise his strongly felt position—and if so,
how to do it. His dilemma lay in truth versus loyalty
(say what you think, or keep still to maintain family
harmony) and in short term versus long term
(say something now, or say it later). His task was
not simply to tell a story but to find a particularly
apt analogy.

- *Some dilemmas have no trilemma options.* If you think
  otherwise, you risk becoming an unconscionable
  compromiser, waffling just when you should have
  stood firm and acquiescing in ways that set at risk
  your commitment to the core values. There are points
  when, in the absence of a true trilemma option, you'll
  be required to take a courageous and even unpleasant
  stand for one side or the other. But even when no
  obvious trilemma appears, the search for it helps you
  give new validity to a word often troubling to young
  people: *compromise.* Some see compromise as a
  synonym for abject surrender, failures of nerve,
  or retreats from rationality to be avoided at all costs.
  Others see compromise as a form of tactful negotiation,
  where the worst aspects of a situation are tamped down
  and the best characteristics allowed to rise to
  prominence. At its best, the compromise in a
  trilemma option arises when somebody puts on
  the table a creative, satisfying, win-win solution.
  Don't assume there will always be one. But don't
  refuse to search.

Did the parable work? "They certainly got the point," Charlie recalls, "and I think it forced them to look harder at their own reasoning processes." What's more, it turned what could have been an unwelcome and uncomfortable discussion into a lively, friendly evening. Charlie did, however, have to confess that to make his ethical point, he had concocted a fiction, using a ruse to unearth a truth. Of such contradictions are good conversations sometimes made.

Lessons from — Finding the Third Way

- In parenting, sometimes less is more. Just because teens are developing their rational capacities doesn't mean you need to go into verbal overdrive.
- Teens appreciate complexity and welcome structures for handling it. Parents can help them grasp trilemma options, where dilemmas have middle-ground solutions.
- Often a brief parable or story, fictional or true, will invite a real interchange among teens—and allow them to make your point for you while you just watch.
- Letting kids put core values on the table saves you from having to do it. When they've said that something really matters, they're more likely to act on it.

A Sexual Crisis

The trilemma option facing Charlie arrived as he struggled to find a way to speak up without giving offense. Once he saw how to make his point, however, it took no particular moral courage for him to go forward.

But what happens when it's clear what you ought to do, and you then have to summon up the courage to do it? That's the situation Cort faced the week after his teenage daughter, Tarn, chose not to sleep with her boyfriend.

Tarn was a junior in high school, and during the months leading up to the prom she had been dating Joe, a senior. The relationship gave Cort and his wife, Melissa, some concern. Joe was a nice enough kid, but he seemed to have a very different set of values—"in fact, no values at all," Cort recalls. In their rural high school, where both Cort and his wife had been teachers, there was an evident social split between what was sometimes described as "the preppie set" and the kids from "the other side of the tracks." Tarn clearly wasn't a classic preppie—she grew up with her parents on a farm where they spent a lot of time doing chores and reading, and where TV was deliberately absent. Joe, by contrast, lived with a single mother who struggled with addictions and was financially insecure. He was "a pretty happy-go-lucky guy," Cort recalled, who was "essentially innocent" despite "the difficulties of his nonfunctioning family." From their years of experience in high school classrooms, Cort and Melissa recognized the relationship they saw developing between their daughter and Joe. And while they didn't much like it, they realized that forbidding their daughter to see Joe could drive the teenagers closer together. So they agreed to say as little as possible and keep a close eye on things.

The weekend of the prom, Cort and Melissa were out of town at a conference. They left clear instructions with Tarn and with an Asian exchange student who was living with them for the semester about what was and wasn't permitted. Midway through their conference, the exchange student left a worried phone message at their hotel alerting them that Tarn was planning to let Joe spend the night at their house. Communications were difficult: Tarn was already caught up in the swirl of events leading to the prom, Cort and Melissa were immersed in their conference, and neither of them had a cell phone. Even if it had been easy to talk, what would they have said? All they could do, says Cort, was to trust Tarn's judgment.

Having the Difficult Discussion

In the end, Tarn decided not to let Joe spend the night. For many parents, that resolution could easily have been such a welcome relief that it would effectively have ended the story. But not for Cort. He doesn't recall directly addressing the issue with Tarn, though he says he probably did. What he remembers is the conviction that he needed to speak to Joe—not that he wanted to, but that he *had* to. So the following Saturday, he went to see Joe at his house. Given that a week had intervened since the prom and that Joe knew Tarn's dad was coming over to talk to him, Cort felt "a little fear and trepidation." After all, how often in a parent's life does this kind of discussion arise? As Cort says, "I hadn't had this kind of conversation with anybody!"

As Cort recalls, it was "one of those kitchen chats—I sat there, and he kind of walked around a bit." It started with some awkward moments as Joe explained that, in essence, hormones were all that mattered. But as they talked, Cort sensed that he was open and friendly, not guarded or secretive. He also realized that nowhere in his upbringing had Joe had any parental guidance on moral issues. So "we just talked about the issue of one's relationships to one's friends," says Cort, "what respect meant, what friendship really was, and about giving and taking and how the friendship could be beneficial to each one." He remembers trying to help Joe see that there were "other options" beside sexual relations, and that "even when you love somebody, there were other ways to act that out than what he had chosen."

"This is a new conversation for him," Cort remembers thinking. As Joe said to him, "I've never talked about this, this way." He just thought sex was "what everybody did when he became a senior in high school." As Cort recalls, it was "extremely cordial, even friendly," and he came away with "a really warm feeling for this young man."

Joe went into the military in another few months, and Tarn broke off the relationship. Even so, Joe continued to call Cort and his wife. "There were some long calls," Cort remembers, where "he would tell us what he was doing and discovering about himself." He later married and had children.

Finding the Courage to Address Uncomfortable Subjects

Woven into this story are genuine flashes of moral courage. We don't know what was going on in Tarn's mind, but she may have been required to take a stand for responsibility (to others) and respect (for herself) as she changed her initial plans for sleeping with Joe. Moral courage is perhaps more obvious in the exchange student. Given the strong peer group strictures about "ratting out" friends and divulging others' secrets, she was caught in a truth-versus-loyalty dilemma. She faced a formidable case for keeping quiet—and an equally persuasive case for sharing the truth with her host family. That she picked up the phone at all tells us something significant about her willingness to take action when her standards were being challenged.

But the clearly courageous actor here is Cort. Since we already know how the story turns out, we're at risk of overlooking that point. After all, how much courage can it take to talk candidly with a teenager? The answer to that question, sadly enough, is not as obvious as it might be. The parenting landscape is littered with the husks of once-strong parent-child relationships shriveled up by failures to speak up forthrightly, affectionately, and quickly. What makes this a story of moral courage is not that lives were in peril, fortunes at risk, or reputations in danger. In fact, Cort wasn't even facing an inescapable obligation, a duty he felt honor-bound to fulfill. Wouldn't many parents in that situation simply have harbored a low-grade resentment for Joe rather than going the extra mile to help him become a better young man? Wouldn't it have been far easier—and probably more socially acceptable—just to let it pass?

But as Cort's story reminds us, having the courage to be moral requires us to take action when our values are put to the test. Expressing moral courage always involves facing down some kind of risk or threat. Taking action may cause lasting, deep-seated challenges and even animosities—a distinct possibility, Cort realized, as he considered whether to talk to Joe. But standing for conscience can also be transformative, not only for the decision maker but for the entire situation. And given our collective yearning for heroes and admirable exemplars, the expression of moral courage may create legacies that outlast the individual experiences—as happened with Joe.

Teaching Others to Stand for Conscience

Yet despite those benefits, the immediate challenge remains: Can we summon up the inner trust and confidence needed to endure danger—or just discomfort—for the sake of principle? Given the tensions of peer loyalty and community allegiance so common among young people, the lens of moral courage leads parents to some of their most important conversations. We don't know whether Cort's example helped Joe deepen and enrich the courage of his own character. We do know that Cort's actions reflect the three modes of learning and teaching that, in an earlier book on moral courage, I identified as the ways moral courage most commonly gets itself embedded in the next generation:

1. *Discourse and discussion*, where the language of rational inquiry clarifies the idea of moral courage and renders it explicable and relevant

2. *Modeling and mentoring*, where real-life exemplars demonstrate moral courage in action and chart pathways of human endeavor that others can follow

3. *Practice and persistence*, where learners can discipline themselves
   through direct, incremental skill building that increases their
   ability to apply moral courage[2]

Foremost among these, in Cort's case, was the second. True,
the discourse itself (point 1) was important: Cort needed to help
Joe see the value of the self-denial he had expressed out of respect
for Tarn. And it certainly took persistence (point 3) for Cort to
seek out Joe—and to fend off the dozens of temptations that must
have arisen to make him want to reconsider, back off, and punt
during that week between the prom and the talk. But the real
teaching in that moment lay in Cort's modeling of the courage to
make the visit at all. That modeling was coupled with the mentoring impulse Cort felt for someone who had to navigate the moral
geography of social interaction unaided and uncoached. That
modeling seems to have been the lesson that stuck with Joe. What
if we could seek him out today and ask him about that conversation? Could Joe remember anything Cort actually had said to him?
Probably not. But could he recall the impact the visit made, the
respect and interest Cort showed for him, the feeling of being
included? I suspect so. I suspect, too, that he recognized that Cort's
actions required real moral courage—and that somewhere inside
him there remains a voice of conscience that now and again says,
"When my kids are that age, I want to be like that man!"

Well, you may be thinking, that's fine for Cort, because it all
turned out well. But what if the results were simply awful? What
if Joe blew him off, eloped with Tarn, and fathered several children
before he deserted her? Would Cort's action still rank as an example
of moral courage? Or would it have simply been an act of foolish
bravura, the failed foray of a white knight who thought he could
save the world?

I'd still chalk it up to moral courage. Had Joe been inclined
toward that kind of grim self-centeredness, it's hard to see how the
pattern of his life would have changed either because Cort showed

up at his house that day or because, having second thoughts, he had not. Cort's intuitions evidently led him to sense a receptivity in Joe that was rewarded. But he had no guarantee that the dangers he faced would be fully met and mastered. If moral courage always allayed every danger and defanged every risk, there would be no real danger to endure, and therefore no courage to be expressed. What defines moral courage is not the success or failure but the effort, the willingness to try, the capacity to hazard action in situations lying well beyond our comfort zone. That, I'm willing to guess, is the lesson Joe took away from that formative visit in his kitchen. And that, I suspect, is why he continued to stay in touch with Cort and Melissa through the years.

Lessons from   **A Sexual Crisis**

- Parenting often goes beyond your own offspring. As teens introduce you to their friends, don't be surprised if they need your help more than your own children do.
- The best parenting is often a quiet expression of moral courage. No one would fault Cort for not speaking up. He knew he had to, and he changed a life.
- Courage gets taught by discussion, modeling, and practice. How you model courage can have impacts you may never know.

Caught Stealing

Joe, you recall, came from the other side of the tracks. Yet a single encounter with an adult in a parent-like situation put him onto a different trajectory.

Leo's background was arguably worse, and the change came more incrementally. But a key moment, Ali recalls, was the day she caught him stealing the granola bars from her pantry.

Leo had been a good friend of Ali's son, Jeb, since the boys were in grade school—frequently visiting after school, sometimes staying overnight, and once even joining the family for Thanksgiving when his own dysfunctional family had hit a particularly rocky patch. He had terrible table manners, she remembers, and wasn't very good at showing gratitude. But he was lively and sharp-witted, and now, as the boys began high school, he seemed more at loose ends than ever before. So it didn't surprise her when he and Jeb would regularly show up at their house after school. A typical afternoon began with them heading straight for the pantry, breaking out the chocolate-covered granola bars, and slathering them with peanut butter for a snack.

On that afternoon, however, something—a phone call, perhaps—had taken Jeb into another room, leaving Leo alone in the kitchen. As Ali came around the corner, Leo was in the pantry, stuffing into his pockets the contents of an entire box of granola bars.

Following Intuition

The story goes on. But pause for a moment, and put yourself in Ali's shoes. What does she do? A range of options is open to her. At one end of the spectrum of moral responses, she could pretend she hadn't seen him—or that, if she had, she hadn't recognized what he was doing. In an instantaneous truth-versus-loyalty calculation, she might have determined that it wasn't worth damaging the loyalty she and Leo felt toward one another by embarrassing him—despite the truth that he was lifting her granola bars. She might well have reasoned that it was better to keep the peace than rock the boat, perhaps promising herself that she would address the situation at a more opportune moment when Jeb (who had stepped away only briefly) wouldn't be present and she could talk quietly and privately to Leo. But would that be ethics, or procrastination? If, like Terri and her can of worms (Chapter Four), she never did speak up, she might berate herself for years for ducking an opportunity to take a moral stand. But if, like Cort in the previous story, she had waited a few days for the proper opportunity, she might find exactly the right moment to help change a young life. Passing by the pantry without a word, in other words, might well represent a noble moral position.

But let's look at the other end of the spectrum. What if, appalled by what she saw as she came around the corner, she burst into a torrent of recrimination? What if her outrage at this violation of her family's trust, this jarring glimpse of a selfish and conniving mind hidden away inside the boy she thought she knew, had flipped her mental switch from passive to active mode? What if her deep desire to correct such misbehavior, once and for all, had led to a firm and authoritarian confrontation? That path might lead to a tough conversation right then and there—with Jeb perhaps present as a stunned and embarrassed witness. It might even have led to expelling Leo from the premises—sent home to think hard about who he was and what kind of relationship he wanted with Ali's family. Taken to an extreme, of course, such a stand becomes unethical. Few would call it right if Ali, in the grip of a wholesale emotional meltdown, had banished him forever from their home in a moment of rage and frustration. But if what Leo needed just then was a stern adult rebuke—not of his individuality, but of the particular behavior he was exhibiting at that moment—might that lead to a significant transformation in his thought? Tough love, many might say—which is also a noble, if harrowing, way for ethics to get done.

What, in fact, did Ali do? Going to neither of these extremes— creating, in a way, her own trilemma option—she found herself doing something that in retrospect seemed to rebuke and comfort at the same time.

"Leo!" she exclaimed as she rounded the kitchen counter, without really having any time to think. "You don't have to do that! You can have as many as you want."

He stopped, sheepishly. "Okay, okay, Mrs. Farmer," he said as he put them back.

As is so often the case in such situations, she had no time to plan what she should do. Her moral intuitions simply took over, guiding her into a situation where two motherly impulses—to defend the family and nurture the needy—came squarely together. Yet in that moment, as she later explained, she sensed that she'd touched on the real problem, which was that in Leo's world, he *couldn't* have as many as he wanted. When he went home, there weren't any there—nor much of anything else he wanted and needed.

"I don't think he was honest with us a lot of the time," she says, "when we tried to ask about things at home. I don't think he told us how it really was."

How Families Build Cultures of Integrity

There are lots of sociological reasons to explain why Leo was attracted to Jeb's house: the sense of kindness, the easy generosity, the reasonable tone to the conversation, the attitude of acceptance, the naturalness of the affection. All that and more produced a culture—a climate, an atmosphere, a tone—that Leo couldn't have defined but couldn't avoid feeling. That climate, in a sense, replaced any need on Ali's part to engage explicitly with our three lenses:

- She didn't articulate any particular core value.
  Although responsibility and respect were obvious
  candidates for a discussion of Leo's obligations and his
  sense of appreciation for the worth of their home, Ali
  never went there.

• She didn't see herself in a right-versus-right dilemma
  needing resolution. While truth versus loyalty could
  have caused her to consider passing by, she apparently
  never gave that a thought. Her moral intuition kicked
  in before she had the chance to reason.

• She probably didn't feel she was expressing any
  notable moral courage. Others, more naturally timid
  or less confident in their relationship with teenagers,
  might describe her immediate and forceful reply as
  courageous. But she herself saw no imminent
  danger that needed to be endured for the sake of
  her principles, and I imagine few observers would
  single this out as a situation where her gutsiness
  deserved praise.

How, then, do you describe Ali's moral situation? Did it have
nothing to do with the lenses of values, dilemmas, and courageous
actions around which this book has been built? In fact, it had
everything to do with them, and all at once.

What Ali and her family had created within their home can
best be described as a culture of integrity. It wasn't a culture of
overt lectures: Ali and her husband don't recall many moments of
deliberate moral teaching or ethical instruction, with either their
own children or outsiders. Instead they had created an atmosphere
determined not so much by *what* they did but *how* they did it—an
atmosphere powerfully appealing for someone whose own home
didn't have it. When Ali said to Leo, "You don't have to do that,"
she was actually saying something far larger: *That's not how we do
things in our house*. And when Leo responded not by running away,
lashing out, or breaking down in tears but by putting everything
back, he seemed to acknowledge that he too wanted to be part of
that culture.

Culture is all about *how we do things around here*—a simple, colloquial phrase that gives us a useful way to define that complex word. Within the home—or more precisely, within the parent-child atmosphere that permeates and characterizes a home—the culture depends on *how we in this family do things with one another and outsiders within our immediate context.* Since *how* is an adverb, whatever parents decide to do could be done harshly, timidly, deceitfully—or ethically, properly, and rightly. The distinction is crucial. Culture is defined less by the things we do than by the way we do things. When the deliberate, settled practice of the family is to do things ethically and morally, then the culture is one of integrity. In that context, the default position for decisions and actions will be to uphold core values, so that the family's *how* is defined as *honestly, responsibly, respectfully, fairly,* and *compassionately.* Notable in our definition, too, is the word *we.* How *I* do things around here is style; how *we* do them is culture. Many a family—and many a business, school, or government agency—has run aground on the shoals of an ego that tried to replace culture with style. As in organizational management, so in parenting, the phrase "my way or the highway" starts, fatally, with the singular pronoun. Culture, by contrast, is a collective endeavor: *our way* doesn't have to end with "or the doorway."

With that in mind, then, it's clear that Ali's response to Leo's would-be heist was not simply her way versus his way. It was *our way*—a kind of collective response from a culture of integrity larger than herself. It was not, as we noted, the result of any particular focus on core values, decision paradigms, or moral courage—for the simple reason that it was the confluence of all three.

Picture a culture of integrity as a planetary center, surrounded by the gravitational pull of our values, our decisions, and our courage (Figure 5.1). Recognize, too, that core values are rooted in our intuitions, decision making is undergirded by rationality, and moral courage requires us to put our values and decisions into action. When a culture of integrity is well expressed, as it is

Figure 5.1 Culture of Integrity

in many well-running families, the forces of intuition, reason, and action are in balance, with no one of them either virtually absent or overwhelmingly present. In such a family, the culture of integrity is almost invisible but immediately tangible, hardly noticed but absolutely inescapable. Not only does it make your own children better ethical actors and your own parenting more integrated, stable, and natural. It also holds up a beacon to the Leos of this world, extending the sphere of influence of a single family in ways often unseen by those who live inside that sphere.

How Family Stories Sustain Family Cultures

Of the many things that create a culture of integrity within families, one of the most important is storytelling—not bedtime stories or tales from books but narratives from within the family itself. Parents are often instinctively aware that at one level, they're steadily laying down the narratives that define where we came from and who we are. Ask Charlie about the impact of that conversation about the radar detector, and he'll tell you that the tale has passed into the family lore. Every once in a while, he says, it gets remembered and retold, as a way through which family members remind one another how they think and what they care about. Ask a contented family member what his family is like—which is really a way of asking about the family culture—and the first thing you'll get are attributes: *kind, generous, zany, energetic,* and so forth. Push deeper, and what pops up are the narratives—"I remember once when we . . . " That's not surprising. Culture lives in the stories we tell about it. The point? What parents and their children do now is potentially vital in creating the stories that set the tone and climate in a household for years to come. How challenges are resolved creates the defining narratives that shape the culture down through history. Over the years, family members revisit those tales as a way of saying either, "Here's a story that shows us who we really are," or "Here's what we need to avoid in the future."

If that's true for culture in general, it's particularly true for the moral culture. As parents and children face and address moral issues, they build the stock of narratives that define family life. That's partly why family photographs are so important. Each one encapsulates a little story, a recollection of the way characters interacted in a particular time and place. Some pictures evoke only one-line comments, while others call forth dense and almost theatrical recollections of feelings, actions, and intentions that have a beginning, a middle, and an end. The pictures that say most, and the narratives that resonate most deeply, are those that carry the strongest moral content—the ones about which family members can most easily say, "The moral of this story is . . . "

For Ali and her family, Leo and his granola bars has become a defining narrative. It tells about a climate of continuing acceptance and patient forgiveness at the Farmers'. It contrasts their culture with the grim world of deprivation and moral vacuum over at Leo's. It speaks to inclusiveness, outreach, and warmth. And it addresses both the risks of putting the Farmers' culture together with Leo's—in a single location, "around here," right in our pantry—and the rewards for doing so.

How did that culture affect Leo? Years earlier, when he was at risk of flunking fourth grade, Ali's husband helped him see that if he didn't pass, his closest friends would leave school and move ahead while he stayed behind. "He hadn't thought of that," said Ali's husband. "He had no idea what the ramifications were of falling behind."

Leo and Jeb stayed close during high school, and Ali often picked Leo up for track meets. He was, she says, "a wonderful athlete." But his own family wouldn't provide transportation to the meets, and she often had to help him do the paperwork to register since he wouldn't do it himself. Yet the very ease with which she expressed herself through her family culture—the same ease with which she had confronted him over the granola bars— raised a crucial and recurring question in Ali's mind: Am I hindering his growth by doing so many things for him, or am I allowing him to succeed during a difficult passage?

Kids Can Overcome Selfishness—and Parents Can Help

Behind that question lies an even deeper one: Was Leo capable of benefiting from a moral influence? Were his intelligence and intuition able to respond to the warmth and affection of a family culture, or was he the end product of a hereditary line so compromised as to be void of moral discernment? Did he come from all the wrong places genetically and biophysically? Was he inherently incapable of applying his understanding of right and wrong in ways that would ever allow him to operate from a basis of values rather than rules, of a moral sense rather than a legal constraint? Was he, in other words, doomed to an inherent selfishness that no amount of care could overcome? Was Ali up against an immovable force that, despite her best efforts, made her efforts pointless?

These questions are not new. Throughout history, the answers to them have been wide and varied. For some, humans are innately moral beings. Thomas Jefferson, for one, thought that man's "sense of right and wrong" was "as much a part of his nature, as the sense of hearing, seeing, feeling. . . . The moral sense, or conscience, is as much a part of man as his leg or arm. It is given to all human beings in a strong or weaker degree, as force of members is given them in a greater or less degree. It may be strengthened by exercise, as may any particular limb of the body." And while this moral sense is "submitted indeed in some degree to the guidance of reason," it is not dependent on intellectual prowess alone. "State a moral case to a ploughman and a professor," Jefferson continues, and "the former will decide it as well, and often better than the latter, because he has not been led astray by artificial rules."[3]

At the other end of the spectrum lie the assertions of gene theory. In his tightly written classic, *The Selfish Gene*, Richard Dawkins argues that "we, and all other animals, are machines created by our genes. Like successful Chicago gangsters, our genes have survived, in some case for millions of years, in a highly competitive world [because] the predominant quality to be expected in a successful gene is ruthless selfishness. This gene selfishness will usually give rise to selfishness in individual behavior. . . . Much as we might like to believe otherwise, universal love and the welfare of the species as a whole are concepts that simply do not make evolutionary sense."[4]

Between these two views, what is Ali to do? One voice points to our moral sense, the other to our ruthless selfishness. With Jefferson at her side, she'd be encouraged to persist in helping Leo's moral sense become "strengthened by exercise." With Dawkins whispering in her ear, however, she may well wonder whether she was up against a primordial "selfishness in individual behavior" over which neither she nor Leo had any real control.

Dawkins himself, however, offers Ali a way forward. "My own feeling," he writes in a moment of personal confession early in the book, "is that a human society based simply on the gene's law of universal ruthless selfishness would be a very nasty society in which to live. . . . [But] be warned that if you wish, as I do, to build a society in which individuals cooperate generously and unselfishly towards a common good, you can expect little help from biological nature. Let us try to *teach* generosity and altruism, because we are born selfish. Let us understand what our own selfish genes are up to, because we may then at least have the chance to upset their designs, something that no other species has ever aspired to."[5]

In this light, Ali's efforts take on a new purpose: she is seeking to confront the genes and "upset their designs." She may think, given the social disparities between Leo and her own family, that the designs most in need of upsetting lie within Leo's genes. In fact, the real focus of her work lies within her own family. Her task is to upset the genetic determinism arguing that neither the "universal love" nor "the welfare of the species" so evidently displayed in the moral culture of her family is relevant to human progress. True, this sense of love and welfare may not make what Dawkins calls "evolutionary sense." In Jefferson's terms, however, it makes perfect "moral sense." And in her own family, where the culture of integrity is so well established, it has already had its impact on Leo. At the time Ali told me her story, Leo was twenty-two years old, working, married, and with a little boy.

"Are you going to be a good dad?" Ali asked him when they happened to meet one day in town.

"Oh, I'm going to try, Mrs. Farmer!" he said.

Suppose he tries—and fails. Suppose, in the end, genes take over. Will Ali's efforts have all been for naught? I don't think so. If, as Jefferson argued, moral exercise strengthens the moral sense, then surely Ali's own family culture is stronger because of the interaction with Leo. This is not an argument for ultimate selfishness, as though Ali's family had simply used Leo as a foil for their own benefit. The moral intention, throughout the process, was always to help Leo prosper. If that taught the family some lessons in compassion, responsibility, and respect, those lessons remain, whatever the ultimate outcome. To argue otherwise would be to dispatch the entire ethical enterprise into a limbo of uncertainty, where no moral progress could be measured because nothing was ever finished. The metaphor in the quote attributed to Jefferson earlier in this chapter is apt: strengthen a limb, or a moral sense, and while it may weaken again through lack of exercise, right now it is undoubtedly stronger than it was just a few days ago. Of such incremental successes is moral development made.

Lessons from   Caught Stealing

- When parents catch kids in bad situations, they can speak up promptly or find a better time to talk. Either way, a brief affectionate rebuke can save the day.
- Families build cultures of integrity—climates of goodness—by the right balance of the three lenses of values, decision making, and moral courage.
- Such cultures are tremendously appealing to outsiders— although sometimes almost invisible to the families that have them.
- Even if kids seem to have a "selfish gene," parents can upset that genetic design, encourage their innate moral sense, and help them overcome ethical limitations.

Confronting Parental Weakness

So far in this book, I've taken a somewhat literal definition of *parenting* as a family relationship involving one's own children or stepchildren.

The prior two stories, however, expanded the palette. Joe wasn't part of Cort's family or Leo of Ali's. In both cases, Cort and Ali were drawn into parenting roles by a kind of vacuum: neither

Joe nor Leo had much effective parenting in his life. While Cort's daughter and Ali's son were central players in those events, the parenting had to extend beyond family relationships. As our next actor learned, however, the issues facing quasi-parents can arise even when your own child is not involved—and when the problem is not a lack of good parenting but a glut of bad parenting.

Reflecting on his thirty years as a scoutmaster in a midwestern city, Chet recalled the only time he ever had to deny a young man the Eagle Scout award—the highest rank a Boy Scout can earn, and one that carries considerable honor. The issue concerned Skipper, a member of Chet's troop and the son of the commissioner of the local Boy Scout Council in whose jurisdiction Chet served. His father, an influential and formidable local citizen, had given his son no choice: Skipper would be an Eagle Scout, full stop.

The young man had started out in the troop doing very well. A good follower, he progressed into a fine leader until he reached the Life rank, just below Eagle. But at that age, his car and his girlfriend loomed large in his life. In addition, he was active in his church's youth group and held a part-time job. "All good things," Chet observed. "But sometimes when a scout gets to that age, scouting has done its job, its function is over, and the young man needs to move on."

Skipper's father didn't see it that way. So over the next year, Skipper dutifully showed up for meetings. But he increasingly treated them as study halls, working on his homework instead of participating in the program. As far as Chet could recall, Skipper didn't take part in a single outside activity that year or attend any of the planning meetings. More tellingly, he never wore his scout uniform. During this time, his peers elected him a senior patrol leader, a role he fulfilled in name only.

"He didn't cause any trouble," Chet was quick to point out. "He was a good, wholesome young man, but he was there only in body, not in spirit. He needed to be able to move on, but he wasn't given that choice."

Taking Advantages

One night during a meeting, Chet's assistant scoutmaster over-heard Skipper explain to a friend that he wasn't really worried about making Eagle Scout because his dad was the commissioner and could, if necessary, go over the scoutmaster's head. In context, it struck the assistant less as a boast than a statement of fact. After that, Chet began keeping careful records of Skipper's activities within the troop. He also counseled him formally on two occasions, reminding him that participating in the meetings, wearing the uniform, and embodying the scouting spirit all factored into the decision-making process for this coveted rank. Skipper assured Chet that things would improve, but nothing changed. His Eagle project appeared, in Chet's eyes, to be little more than "a day of fun and games," with no serious service or work component.

When at last the young man showed up to get the scoutmaster's signature on his Eagle Scout application, Chet sat him down and explained why he couldn't recommend him. The young man listened, said that he understood, and noted that he didn't have a problem with the decision.

"But you know," he added, "there's going to be a fight from my dad."

That's exactly what happened. Within a few days, Chet got a letter informing him that in place of the local board of review typically assembled to approve Eagle Scout candidates, a special council-appointed board was being impaneled, presided over by a local circuit court judge active in scouting. Both sides were invited to present their cases.

Unraveling Complexity

What should Chet do? Should he stand up to a powerful and politi-cally sophisticated opponent who was also his boss? Or should he reconsider his objection and preserve his position as scoutmaster? If he fought and lost, he would almost certainly lose his post—and with it the opportunity to work with other scouts, now and in the future. And loss seemed almost certain. "I knew that if I took the bull by the horns," he said, "I could never let go, because he would smash me into the ground." But if he looked the other way—hoping, perhaps, that Skipper would improve over the years and dignify the rank he would certainly be awarded—he would have failed, as he said, to "uphold the honor of the Eagle" and everything that scouting stood for.

At that point, Chet found himself facing, all at once, the three frameworks we've been talking about in this book: the values involved in knowing what's right, the dilemma resolution process needed in making tough choices, and the moral courage required in standing for conscience:

- *Knowing what's right.* Even if Chet's understanding of ethics had extended only to the five shared values, he would still have had a firm basis for beginning to analyze his situation. Honesty would have counseled him to make an unvarnished, impersonal assessment of Skipper's performance—and responsibility would have told him to stick with that assessment despite pressure to capitulate. Fairness might have been slightly less clear. While it would surely be fair to every other scout to uphold common standards, was it fair to refuse to sign Skipper's forms? Or should he go the extra mile—giving him a chance to redo his Eagle project, perhaps, or participate in a few more troop meetings? Compassion could certainly argue for the latter course. And as for respect, Chet knew the importance of dignifying the uniform and the rank structure of the scouts by obeying those in command. So while those values certainly helped Chet think through his options, they sounded an uncertain trumpet. Had a friend counseled Chet to just "obey his values"—a sadly common piece of advice these days, oversimplifying the moral rationality required to address complex dilemmas—he would have been left without a clear direction. Why? Because while a simple values analysis is appropriate for right-versus-wrong temptations, it fails to satisfy the intellectual and moral demands posed by right-versus-right dilemmas.

- *Making tough choices.* The dilemma Chet faced—to hold his ground or accede to the commissioner—pulled him in opposite directions. As a short-term-versus-long-term dilemma, it presented him with two untenable options. If he stood his ground to defend the long-term value of the Eagle Scout rank, he and his troop would almost surely suffer in the short term. If he protected his troop and his position in the here-and-now, however, he would not only degrade the long-term worth of the Eagle rank but send the remaining troop members a chilling message about adult compromise. Also on the table was the tension of truth telling ("Skipper isn't qualified") versus loyalty (obeying the chain of command), as well as the good of the entire scouting community versus the importance of satisfying one individual and his son. And as an examination of Chet's values would have made clear, there was also a justice-versus-mercy component. Knowing that he had to stand for a principled sense of fairness, he nevertheless wondered (as we all do) whether he had done all he could to help this young man reach his goal. How to resolve those tensions? Through an ends-based principle, Chet could easily see that the greatest good for the greatest number might well be for his scouts to benefit from the continuity of their longtime scoutmaster rather than making them unwitting pawns in a nasty and personal battle raging above their heads. But through a rule-based

principle, he could understand that if, from now on,
every scoutmaster in every troop permitted shoddy
performance among Eagle Scout applicants, the result
would be devastating for the future of scouting. As for
the care-based principle, he could see the Golden Rule
encouraging him either to do what Skipper said he
wanted (sign the form) or what he really may have
wanted (escape from his father's pressure)—a point on
which I'll have more to say in a moment.

- *Standing for conscience.* In the end, Chet knew
  what was right: Skipper wasn't qualified, and it was
  appropriate to prevent him from attaining the Eagle
  Scout rank. But knowing what's right is very different
  from having the moral courage to do it. As is often the
  case in right-versus-right dilemmas, one side requires
  far more courage than the other. Had Chet concluded
  that he had to pass Skipper along, no further courage
  would have been required. He might have faced bouts
  of self-condemnation and remorse, but he wouldn't
  have needed to take a public stand for a moral choice.
  Choosing the other side, however, required significant
  moral courage—a willingness to endure danger for the
  sake of principle. What dangers could he foresee?
  Clearly he would see the obvious external ones
  involving harm to the troop if he were expelled from
  his post. As with many other morally courageous
  actions, he also faced more subtle arguments. First, did
  he really know enough to make this decision, stand up
  to a circuit court judge, and defend his position? Fear
  of ambiguity—"Maybe I don't have all the facts; maybe
  I should wait until it gets clearer"—would disable
  many morally courageous actions. Second, was he
  really willing to be out in front on this one, find

his reputation under attack, and take the public recrimination that might arise from opposing a canny and powerful public figure? Third, was he inviting significant personal loss—not of pay or career, since this was a volunteer position, but of his affection for scouting, his commitment to the young men with whom he worked, and the motivation that had kept him going when it might have been just as easy to quit? These were not simple calculations. Each one could have derailed him. His moral courage, then, had to be expressed not only in standing up against the objective and obvious dangers in this situation, but in subduing the nagging inner doubts that so often arise in such situations.

Overcoming the Temptation to Walk Away

In the end, Chet stood his ground. Although he had an option most parents don't have—he could have walked away from this quasi-parenting role in a heartbeat simply by tendering his resignation—he chose to fight it out. After due deliberation, the council review board agreed with his position, but Skipper's father then appealed to the national council in Texas. When that board upheld the local council's decision, the father pulled out the heavy artillery and threatened legal action. As it happened, however, he never made good on the threat, which fell hollowly to the ground. Skipper is not now, and never was, an Eagle Scout.

One afternoon years later, Chet caught sight of Skipper in the city, at some distance. When Skipper spotted him, he came directly over, greeted him warmly, and talked easily and naturally about his activities. There was no animosity and no mention of the Eagle Scout case. That meeting confirmed what Chet had begun to suspect during the flurry of events years before: that while Skipper had been forced to side with his dad and apply for Eagle Scout ranking, he had always respected Chet's decision and his willingness to stand up for it.

Back, then, to the Golden Rule. As Chet's story reminds us, it can be seductively easy to interpret the care-based principle as meaning, "Always do to others what they appear to be saying they would like you to do." If we really put ourselves solidly in the others' shoes, however, looking out from their eyes and feeling the world as they feel it—and the care-based principle demands nothing less—we're forced to conclude that there are moments when we too would want someone to bring us up short, hold us firmly to the rules, and keep us from taking a path that we were beginning to suspect we no longer wanted to pursue.

It was plain that Skipper never cared much for Eagle Scout status. Maybe, in fact, he didn't care to be one at all but found himself trapped by an authoritarian parent. Chet's story gives us a helpful refinement of the Golden Rule: "Do what's best for others, just as you would have them do what's best for you."

Lessons from   ## Confronting Parental Weakness

- If you're not the parent—and don't even have a child involved—it may seem easy to walk away. But that may be when the world most needs your parenting skills.
- When problems seem entangled and fear looms large, trust the process. Take the situation through the three lenses, and notice how that effort brings clarity.
- The Golden Rule isn't about doing what it appears that others want. Sometimes it's about doing what's best for others because that's what you'd want done to you.
- Building ethics is a long-term endeavor. Sometimes it can be years before you learn that what you stood for made a real difference in another person's life.

Explaining Divorce

Of the challenges Chet encountered, suddenness wasn't one of them. He could see the Eagle Scout problem coming from miles away, and it took more than a year to arrive.

Contrast that pace with the following letter from a colleague describing his divorce. What do you do when a well-meaning question from someone you love suddenly comes out of nowhere, demands an immediate answer, and lands you in a moral pickle?

When Bob's daughter, Nikki, was three years old, his wife began an affair with a longtime family friend—someone Nikki had known her entire life. "This affair," Bob wrote me, "led to our divorce. My ex-wife kept custody of our daughter. Ultimately my wife married the other man, and while my daughter and I stayed very close, her household consisted of her mom and her mom's husband. They had the day-to-day responsibility of raising her."

"When my daughter was a teenager," Bob continues, "she had the typical sorts of adolescent struggles girls have with their mothers. It was not easy for her mom to deal with my daughter's search for boundaries, but—as in all other aspects of her role as mother—I have nothing but praise for the way she raised our daughter. I was careful never to give my daughter the impression that she could count on me to take her side against her mom. On the other hand, I tried to be honest with my daughter about tough subjects like sex, drugs, teen friendships, money, and any other issue she was wrestling with."

One summer when she was about fifteen, he recalls, she came to Bob's for one of her usual extended visits. As they talked freely over their days together, Bob heard a lot about Nikki's mom, her stepdad, her household, and her struggles. But a question from Nikki one day caught Bob unprepared. She'd never asked it before, and suddenly there it was.

"Dad," she said, "why did you and Mom get divorced?"

Bob was pretty sure, he recalled, that he had "never asked her mother what she had told our daughter about this, if anything." He was absolutely sure that he had never discussed it with Nikki. So what does he say? Does he recount her mother's adultery to a girl already at odds with her mom? Or does he fall back on an explanation less forthright but less volatile? We'll get to his reasoning in a moment. First, however, a note about context.

Divorce in America

By the early 1990s, when Bob's marriage dissolved, the divorce rate in the United States had already completed its giddy statistical climb from 2.0 divorces per 1,000 people in 1940 to 5.3 in 1977. More recent data from the National Center for Health Statistics (NCHS), which gathers the figures reported here, shows it stabilizing at about 4.0. Does that mean, as is popularly believed, that 50 percent of today's marriages end in divorce? The NCHS officially answers, "We don't know." As statisticians recognize, this is a complex issue, made all the more so by the need to distinguish separations from divorces, account for family dissolution among adults who were never married in the first place, and track breakups among second and third marriages. But whatever the number, it's substantial.

But it's not the source of social tut-tutting that it once was. In 2008, Gallup reports, 70 percent of Americans thought divorce was morally acceptable—up from 59 percent as recently as 2001. In gathering these figures for its annual Values and Beliefs Survey, Gallup puts divorce in the context of sixteen other issues, asking respondents to rate them as "morally acceptable" or "morally wrong." The trend toward acceptance of divorce has been so strong that it now tops Gallup's list of morally acceptable issues. According to Gallup editor Lydia Saad, it was also the only issue measured in 2008 "for which public opinion has changed to a significant degree over the past year," continuing to move upward toward greater approval.

There is, however, something slightly ironic about that trend. Describing other issues on Gallup's list, Saad points out that tolerance for divorce is statistically close to the public's expression of tolerance for "gambling, the death penalty, embryonic stem-cell research, and premarital sex." Yet "married men and women having an affair is tied with polygamy in last place, and ranks just slightly below cloning humans and suicide in perceived moral acceptability." Hence the irony: divorce is fine, but a leading cause of divorce is repugnant. "Notably," Saad continues, "one of the main reasons many couples seek divorce—because one or both spouses have had an extramarital affair—is at the bottom [of the list]."

Bob hadn't been reading Gallup's statistics when Nikki popped her question. Nor was Nikki aware (as far as Bob could tell) that she was potentially asking a question about adultery. But that didn't change the zeitgeist in which she found herself. If in 2008 more than 90 percent of the public finds "married men and women having an affair" to be morally wrong—and those are Gallup's figures—one can only speculate that the moral opprobrium was at least as strong as, and perhaps stronger than, when Bob discovered his wife's adultery.

Compounding Bob's problem was another issue, flagged by the Gallup Youth Survey in 2003. "Generally speaking," Gallup asked American teens, "do you think it is too easy or not easy enough for people in this country to get divorced?" More than three-quarters (77 percent) answered that it was too easy. Teens, it seems, see an awful lot of divorce around them and would like to see a lot less. In fact, as acceptance of divorce has peaked, teenage concerns about it seem to have risen as well. When Gallup first asked this question of teens in 1977, only 55 percent said it was too easy.

Little wonder, then, that Bob was on alert when Nikki asked her question. Admittedly, he's not like most other Americans: an academic in the field of media studies, he's a sophisticated user and interpreter of survey data. But his responses to these questions

would probably track pretty well with those of the survey respondents. His work with students, including his own daughter, made
him aware that patterns of divorce form a large part of the social
and moral wallpaper behind their young lives. If Nikki were like
her peers, she too would think there's too much divorce on the
landscape. And as much as she might countenance sex outside
marriage—which, by 2008, was thought to be morally acceptable
by more than 60 percent of Gallup's respondents—she probably
would have a decidedly low tolerance for a married woman having
an affair. Given her ongoing struggles with her mom, did Bob
want to exacerbate the mother-daughter frictions by detailing her
mother's behavior?

What Are You *Really* Asking?

From one point of view, he could see, the question Nikki was
asking was straightforward: What caused the breakup? But as a
parent, he needed to be alert that the real question sometimes
lies hidden behind the original question, especially as children
move through adolescence. In Bob's case, the question behind the
question could have taken many forms:

- Who's to blame for the divorce?

- Did you do something terrible to Mom?

- Did she do something terrible to you?

- Was I the cause of your breakup?

- What am I to think of my stepfather?

- Am I doomed to a harder life because of your divorce?

On that last question, a good deal of ink has been spilled.
Reporting on earlier research, Paul Amato and Bruce Keith examined ninety-two studies involving thirteen thousand children.

Their 1991 review concluded that "on average," children from divorced families fared somewhat worse in school, and in life, than children living in intact families.[6]

Assessing this study in 2009, University of Illinois researcher Robert Hughes Jr. found that "these children have more difficulty in school, more behavior problems, more negative self-concepts, more problems with peers, and more trouble getting along with their parents"—findings that continued to be borne out in a later review published in 2001.[7] Hughes cautions, however, that "average differences do not mean that *all* children in divorced families are worse off than *all* children in intact families." In fact, he noted, Paul Amato has estimated that about 40 percent of young adults from divorced families were "doing better than the young people from non-divorced families."[8]

Where, then, was Nikki? Family researchers cite six common risks that, if she had been "average," could have threatened her:[9]

1. Parental loss, or loss of contact with one parent

2. Economic loss, or a diminution of financial resources

3. More life stress, resulting from changes in schools, child care, homes, and so forth

4. Poor parental adjustment, reflecting the mental health of the parents

5. Lack of parental competence in the skills that will help children develop

6. Exposure to conflict between parents, both before and after divorce

In fact, she was well placed to resist each risk: she remained close to Bob, endured no financial hardship, was not buffeted by changes in her life situation, lived in a mentally well-adjusted home, had competent parenting, and experienced little if any conflict between her birth parents. That didn't mean, however, that she wasn't subject to some turmoil over the divorce. In a 2000 study, Laumann-Billings and Emery reported that young adults in their early twenties who had experienced the divorce of their parents still reported "pain and distress" over the breakup ten years later. Researchers also find that children who experience a divorce feel a loss of control over their lives, particularly when they were never brought into the discussions. One study, for example, finds that fewer than 20 percent of children report that both parents talked to them about the impending divorce, and only 5 percent were given any explanation for the change or invited to ask questions.[10]

Back, then, to Nikki's question. What should Bob say?

"I felt that I was confronted with a dilemma that many divorced parents face," Bob's letter continues. It was, as he recognized, a classic tension between truth and loyalty—one of our four paradigms. "I felt tempted to be honest about this question, especially since I felt that I had done the right thing," he writes. "I also felt that my daughter might learn the story eventually from any of her aunts and uncles, and that if I gave a different account now she might doubt me about other difficult subjects in the future."

"I also felt obligated to be loyal to my ex-wife by guarding her privacy and dignity," he continued. "While I had no particularly warm feelings for my ex-wife's husband, I also felt that it would be unwise to diminish him in my daughter's eyes. I could see no advantage to my daughter, especially at this stage of her life, in having information she could throw at her mom in an argument, or information that would diminish the moral authority of the adults in her home."

Answering the Real Question

Facing those two powerful but contrary moral positions, Bob found himself moving toward a kind of trilemma. "The gist of what I told my daughter," he recalls, "was that I had left her mother because we had realized that we didn't share the same understanding of marriage and what it committed us to. I went on to compare that basic situation to relationships my daughter had had with boy-friends who had pressured her for more commitment or attention than she cared to give them. I also compared it to the ever-shifting allegiances among her circle of teen girlfriends. As I often did, I tried to explain how the things she was experiencing in adoles-cence were often small-scale lessons in more substantial problems she would almost surely encounter when she was older (or at least hopefully wouldn't encounter until she was older)." While those analogies might seem a bit obtuse—and might well have come apart under serious questioning from Nikki—the result was just as Bob had hoped: this line of discourse "distracted her from pressing for more details about her mom and me, in favor of focusing on her own experiences."

In the end, then, Bob was able to answer without providing details. "It was most literally true that it was I who moved out of our home—and if my daughter had wanted to interpret that to mean that I had abandoned her and her mother, I would have been willing to clear that up as best I could." In fact, it never came up, because the conversation never continued.

And that raises a profound moral point. Was Bob being com-pletely honest? In logic, three rules of evidence must be observed: it must be accurate, complete, and relevant. When the bailiff asks the witness in the courtroom to swear that she is telling "the truth, the whole truth, and nothing but the truth," he is not only asking whether the testimony is accurate ("the truth") but whether it is also complete ("the whole truth"). Crucially he is asking in addi-tion whether it is entirely relevant to the case at hand ("nothing but the truth")—not surrounded by unrelated statements that, though accurate and complete, are intended to obfuscate, confuse, or distract from the point at issue.

Bob's reply was not dishonest. But was it complete? Perhaps so, as far as it went—though he was apparently ready to flesh out the completeness had he been asked. Yet was it relevant? He was sharp enough to see that a fifteen-year-old girl, invited to discuss her own life rather than the history of her parents, might well take the bit between her teeth and go galloping off into a new line of questioning. In fairness, he may have been asking a fundamental question of her in turn: *Do you seriously want to engage in this conversation right now, because you have deep issues you need to resolve, or is this a somewhat idle query?* Hearing no follow-up, could he be blamed for letting the matter lie?

These are not easy issues. Honesty, at its purest, demands complete candor and straightforwardness. Yet compassion, which in this case was a driver of Bob's loyalty, reminds us that words, mishandled, become weapons. Philosophically and metaphysically, we're under no obligation to blurt out everything we know about every issue any time someone asks—a point universally understood by lawyers obeying attorney-client privilege, journalists protecting their sources, human relations professionals holding employee health records in strict confidence, and priests in the confession booth. If, to avoid the suspicion that we're withholding information, we exercise tact and choose our words carefully, are we being dishonest?

In the abstract, the question is probably unanswerable. Honesty arises in human relationships, each one of which uniquely possesses, as Shakespeare noted, "a local habitation and a name." But even here there are differing ethical traditions. Ends-based thinkers, looking to consequences, will easily exonerate Bob, while Kantians, insisting on universal principles, may take exception to his effort. Through all of this, I'm reminded of a wonderfully wise woman who, in a moment of candor, said to me, "I never have to lie—I have too big a vocabulary."

Bob has no doubt that he did the right thing. He knows that when the time is right for Nikki—perhaps when the spats with her mom have abated or when she's no longer living at home—he'll have that conversation with her and fill her in on whatever she needs to know. At the time, however, he was "careful to avoid blaming anyone or setting up her mom for a confrontation over facts."

His conclusion? "Loyalty to an ex-spouse may be one of the hardest values to practice," he muses, "but I've never regretted making that hard choice in the situation I've described, or in a handful of others when I weighed the interest of my daughter against my own."

Lessons from   Explaining Divorce

- Whether or not you've been divorced, your parenting puts you into contact with a lot of children of divorced parents who may face various risks and need your love.
- Children may pop questions that catch you off guard. Take time to uncover the question behind the question rather than answering right away.
- Sometimes children ask for more than they need to know. Be prepared to explain fully, but avoid arming them with weapons that could hurt them and others.
- Loyalty to an ex-spouse can be tough to feel and hard to maintain. But it can be a powerful form of forgiveness. Your own balance shows kids how to find their own.

6

Ages Nineteen Through Twenty-Three

The toughest job for parents is not to be one—especially as their children approach full adulthood. As children move into their twenties—even, in one story in this chapter, into their thirties—their sense of independence expands at warp speed. In what is typically about a four-year span, they get driver's licenses, form deep relationships with the opposite sex, hit voting age, and gain legal access to bars and clubs. Many of them move from high school regimentation to university laissez-faire, while others advance from part-time jobs into full-time participation in the labor market. And while a large number remain in the parental home—especially during a sagging economy—many move into apartments and homes of their own. It all seems to happen in a blaze of suddenness.

Parents move at no such pace. To many of them, parenting is parenting, no matter the age of the children. What worked a few years ago should continue working today. That attitude shouldn't surprise us. To a forty year old, four years is only a scant 10 percent of one's experience, a tithe of one's time—while to a sixteen year old, it's an eternity, a full quarter of one's lifetime. Add to that the fact that by the time the last child finishes high school, parenting may have lost its luminous sheen of discovery. By that time, the most recently read parenting book has probably sat unopened for years, and nothing new has been added to the shelf. In this circumstance, parenting can come to seem more defensive than offensive, more goal keeping than stick handling, more cruise control than manual.

Attentive parents are alert to this change in their own feelings. Sensing the disparity between the accelerating trends of youth and the braking inclinations of maturity, they recognize that their ethical parenting skills need to adapt as their children grow. From a social perspective, they find themselves adopting a less hands-on approach. Offering guidance only when asked, they're more willing to help kids frame issues than to lay down their own solutions. They find themselves moving gradually from a superior, top-down, vertical view of the parent-child relationship toward a more equalized, evenhanded, horizontal vision. In the moral realm, they find themselves more discursive and less directive, more willing to share their wisdom than to decree an outcome. If parents have educated themselves to address the three lenses put forward in this book—knowing what's right, making tough choices, and standing for conscience—they'll be ready for this new phase in their parenting.

They've been preparing for this phase by watching their children mature within the context of these lenses. They've noticed that what seemed at age three to be an indistinct moral blur became, for their eight year old, a values-driven habit of mind. What their nine year old saw as a black-and-white, right-and-wrong world suddenly, to their fifteen year old, had become an array of right-versus-right ethical dilemmas. And what was paralyzingly scary for their sixteen year old appeared to their college junior as a demand for moral courage. That accumulated wisdom has prepared them for the central role they can play in their children's moral development during their final years in the nest. They can now help young adults recognize and inhabit the universe of shared values without lathering on the valuespeak that so many teens find off-putting. They can frame unruly situations as right-versus-right dilemmas without spouting imperatives or giving commands. They can foster moral courage by appealing to the nobler sentiments of self-respect and altruism without shaming a child into taking a stand for which he or she is unprepared. They can, in other words, gradually and gracefully relinquish capital-P Parenting and take up a new role as wise, thoughtful moms and dads.

Counseling, Not Controlling

Or at least they wish they could. As Cynthia discovered, backing off wasn't easy. When children hit their teenage years, she told us, "Parents have done all the teaching they can." At that point, she said, it's their job to share the wisdom that comes from experience by helping the young adult "make an informed decision, not by telling him or her what to do." What worries her, however, is that this is exactly what she did not do when her nineteen-year-old son, David, came to her with a grueling dilemma. Instead, she blurted out her position before he had even finished explaining the situation. In the end, it turned out well. What still troubles her, however, is a simple question: Did he make the decision, or did I make it for him?

Backing Off

David had just finished high school when he was asked to help coach the school's water polo team. He wasn't much older than many of the boys on the team, and he knew a number of them well. As the season progressed, he gradually became aware that one of the other coaches, an assistant coach one level above him and just a few years older, was supplying marijuana to team members and smoking it with them. David knew the arguments about marijuana. Its proponents saw it as a cheap, commonplace social accessory. To them it was only a matter of time before it was legalized. Its opponents viewed it as a gateway drug to harder stuff and were happy to see it remain an illegal substance. He himself felt no ambivalence: to him, using it was wrong, especially in an athletic context that took an unyielding stand against alcohol and tobacco.

While he felt certain that the head coach was unaware of what was happening, David nevertheless had ample reason to ignore what he was seeing. The assistant coach, who was doing a fine job and getting winning results, had been with the team for several years and commanded the respect of the head coach. David was just starting out. With a desire to protect his reputation for the sake of future positions but with no coaching record to fall back on, he felt particularly vulnerable. Besides, this wasn't about crack or crystal meth or even steroids, which have proved so troubling to professional and amateur sports in recent years. This was, as some of David's classmates used to point out, "just pot, man!"

What, then, was his role? What should he do?

To Cynthia's credit, he turned to her. She had built such a solid relationship with her son that, even at nineteen, he sought out her advice and counsel. As he poured out his tale, she knew she needed to be in listening mode. Yet before she knew it, she was thundering toward her answer. He had no choice, she told him, but to go to the head coach and tell him what was going on. "That's what life is, doing the right thing," she told him. "Otherwise you're not being true to yourself and living by any sense of ideals."

Pause with me here to consider her response. It's clear that David faced a situation that in his mind was unethical. In the realm of right versus wrong, it was distinctly the latter, a straight-forward moral temptation. Yet he nevertheless faced a right-versus-right dilemma—not about the pot smoking but about his response to it. When David came to Cynthia to talk about the *dilemma*, however, Cynthia responded by addressing the *temptation*. We could fault her for that—as she herself, in hindsight, clearly did. But would we be right to do so? Or are there some situations in which the firm articulation of the high moral ground—a forceful rejection of the temptation—actually encourages the decision maker to take the right step, where remaining silent might prolong the decision-making process? Is it true that whenever we face a right-versus-right dilemma, we must immediately shy away from talking about the rightness of our core values and the wrongness of the antivalues? Or can clear statements of moral principle find their proper place even when the discussion needs to turn to right versus right?

Why It's Valuable to Articulate Moral Benchmarks

Some fascinating recent research by Duke University behavioral economist Dan Ariely, one of the coauthors of the counterfeit sunglasses experiment discussed in Chapter One, suggests that it may not only be safe to articulate such values but positively helpful to do so. His work studies the effect that a simple reminder of core values can have on the decision-making process. Characteristically, however, his experiments come at this question sideways, with the participants thinking he's testing their basic prowess in math. He typically asks participants a number of questions like the following: "Look at your watch, note the time, and start searching for two numbers in the matrix [it's in Figure 6.1] that will add up to exactly 10. How long did it take you?"[1]

If you stared at the matrix for a while before finding 4.81 and 5.19, join the group: the answers don't come without some head scratching. But when Ariely and his colleagues brought students together in a lab at UCLA a few years ago, they weren't satisfied with just one such puzzler. They had twenty. The participants were given five minutes to solve as many as they could. As an incentive, they were told they would be entered into a lottery when they

1.69	1.82	2.91
4.67	4.81	3.05
5.82	5.06	4.28
6.36	5.19	4.57

Figure 6.1   Sample Matrix Worksheet

finished and that the lottery winner would get ten dollars for each correct answer.

As you may have suspected, the point of the test was not simply to test math skills. In fact, the participants were divided into two groups. One group handed in their papers directly to the experimenter, while the other simply handed in a sheet with the number of solved problems written on it but without the accompanying test papers. "These participants, obviously, were the ones with the opportunity to cheat," writes Ariely—which, sadly but unsurprisingly, many did. Those with no opportunity to cheat solved, on average, 3.1 problems correctly. Those who could cheat said, on average, that they'd solved 4.1. That they didn't cheat a lot —reporting scores only about 33 percent higher than average— reminds us of Victoria Talwar's experiments (see Chapter One) with "fully skilled lie tellers" who know how to cover their tracks and avoid the appearance of lying.

But even that's not the point of this experiment. Before these participants began the test, they were divided in still another way. Half were asked to write down the names of ten books they're read in high school. The other half was asked to write down "as many of the Ten Commandments as they could recall." Result? Those who had no opportunity to cheat reported 3.1 problems solved, no matter which question they'd been asked. Those who had written down their high school reading lists and had the opportunity to cheat did in fact cheat. And the others? "The results," Ariely reports, "surprised even us: the students who had been asked to recall the Ten Commandments had not cheated at all. They averaged three correct answers—the same basic score as those that could not cheat."[2]

Does this mean that the Ten Commandments help you raise your ability in math? Some follow-up experiments disproved that hypothesis. When there was never an opportunity to cheat, scores of those who had been asked to remember the Commandments were identical to those who had not. Nor, in the original test, did it matter how many Commandments a student could remember: "Students who could remember only one or two Commandments were as affected by them as those who remembered nearly all ten." To explain that effect, Ariely hypothesized that "it was not the Commandments themselves that encouraged honesty, but the mere contemplation of a moral benchmark of some kind."

To test that hypothesis, Ariely set up one last experiment, this time at MIT. Here, as before, some participants had the chance to cheat and others did not. But some in the "could cheat" category were asked to sign a statement before they began, which simply read, "I understand that this study falls under the MIT honor system." Others in the group were not asked to sign anything. The result? Those who did not sign cheated, while those who signed did not. "In other words," Ariely concludes, "when we are removed from any benchmarks of ethical thought, we tend to stray into dishonesty. But if we are reminded of morality at the moment we are tempted, then we are much more likely to be honest."[3] Interestingly, the reminder need be only about a perceived moral benchmark. In this case, as Ariely notes wryly, MIT doesn't even have an honor code.

What does all this have to do with David and the pot-packing coach? Go back to Cynthia's assertion that "that's what life is, doing the right thing," since "otherwise you're not being true to yourself and living by any sense of ideals." While her statement is not exactly a commandment, it's more than a mere recognition of an honor code. It provided for David what Ariely might call one of the "benchmarks of ethical thought" that make it harder for us to "stray into dishonesty." While we don't know the history of Cynthia's relationship with her son, it seems unlikely that this was the first time she had ever articulated such a moral injunction. Chances are she'd returned to these kinds of statements with some frequency. That might make her sound like a hellish moralizer, offering up just the sort of platitudinous repetition that drives teens right out the door. For David, however, it may have provided just the comfort and assurance he needed—a reminder that a moral order did in fact exist and that it was okay to act in accordance with broadly understood standards of integrity.

Examining Scenarios to Make Right Choices

The fact that David hadn't fled from, but in fact had sought out, such moral discourse should give heart to parents who are afraid to speak up about ethical issues. Too often parents are spooked by moral relativism and led to imagine that all moral discourse is mere moralizing. Too often, disenchanted by the hypocrisy of some who preach without practice, parents may let themselves believe that any assertion of rightness is simply proof of self-righteousness. Ariely's findings tell us something else: that a well-placed reminder of a moral benchmark can have a significant positive effect on ethical behavior. Speaking up forcibly for what's right, even in the context of a right-versus-right dilemma, may have a far more encouraging effect than we sometimes think.

How, then, did David resolve his dilemma? Cynthia urged him to consider a number of possible scenarios—because, she said, that's how she tends to think. Even when she's clear on what should be done—in this case, reporting the situation to the head coach—she finds that proposing and examining a range of possible outcomes helps her children recognize the consequences of a decision, whichever way it goes. She feels it also helps them face up to the fact that others may not understand or appreciate what they've done, even if—or especially when—it was the right thing to do.

The first possible scenario proposed that David go directly to the assistant coach—the one supplying the pot. The man was someone David liked, who had once coached him. David had every reason to sit down quietly and persuade him to mend his ways. But would that really bring about change? Could he effectively talk someone out of a drug habit? Even if he could—even if the reefers vanished forever—would the assistant, knowing that David knew about the issue, find ways to ease him out of his position in order to protect his own reputation? Would speaking up change their relationship forever, without any promise that the situation on the ground would change one bit?

In another scenario, David could approach the young swimmers themselves. He could urge them to tell the assistant they were no longer interested in lighting up with him. But unless they whole-heartedly agreed and acted as a bloc—something he suspected wouldn't happen—he could foresee difficulties. What if the assistant coach sought to penalize those who objected and promote those who were still part of his in-group? Then, too, David realized that the team members themselves could be implicated, and possibly kicked off the team, if they admitted to pot smoking and word of it ever got out—a situation, David felt, that would make it even more unlikely that they would agree to speak up.

In yet another scenario, David could take the story to the news media. But while that would certainly clean up the team, it might also destroy it. The result could be a team disbanded, a head coach sacked along with his assistant, and David's own position elimi-nated. He could see a role for the media if, say, the school were infested by mobsters demanding protection money, or if senior administrators were fraudulently inflating athletic qualifications. In this case, however, calling in the reporters seemed a heavy-handed and blunt instrument to use when something more delicate might work just as well.

That left the scenario of going to the head coach. David felt he knew the man to be an honest and caring individual. But he still worried that by going over the assistant's head, the young men he was coaching would refuse to work with him and that this group of friends would never speak to him again.

Whatever the level of influence from his mother, David mustered the courage to talk to the head coach. In other words, he willingly endured significant risk for the sake of his principles— our definition of moral courage. After making a few phone calls to confirm what David had shared, the coach thanked him for coming forward—and fired the assistant coach. Then, to David's surprise and great relief, the members of the team, even those who had been implicated, also expressed their appreciation. Each found a way to come up to David, shake his hand, and say in essence, "Thanks a lot for getting us out of this!" Far from losing his friends, he gained their respect.

Counseling, Not Controlling

- Kids seem to develop at warp speed, but parenting can get caught in ruts. As kids mature, good moral parenting becomes more discursive and less directive.
- But don't be silent. When parents articulate moral benchmarks—reminding kids of ethical standards—that brief reminder can have an immediate, positive impact.
- Teens often see things they wish they hadn't—say, drugs in a locker room. Parents, like coaches, can counsel. But it's the teen who swims the race.
- When your teens take stands for conscience, don't be surprised if other kids thank them for doing it. Teens value standards and respect those who uphold them.

Supporting Your Daughter or Saving Your Grandchildren

If Cynthia feared that she'd been too directive with her teenage son, Fran regretted that she'd been too naive with her unmarried daughter. The challenges began when, on her nineteenth birthday,

Alice announced to her parents that she was pregnant. From there, the issues escalated into the toughest ethical dilemma Fran and her husband had ever faced.

A Surprising Pregnancy

Growing up, neither Alice nor her three siblings had caused any problems for their parents. And why would they? To all appearances, they were raised in an admirable family atmosphere. Fran, who taught elementary school, had spent eighteen years as a paid minister in her church in their southern city. She and her husband were on the same wavelength about raising children, and both were deeply involved in community activities.

"We were the perfect church parents and youth-group advisors," Fran recalls, "and everybody's kids loved us. Ours was the neighborhood's 'everybody-hangs-out-at house' when they were growing up."

"We weren't exactly the Cleavers," she chuckles, invoking the iconic 1950s television sitcom, _Leave It to Beaver,_ about the idealized suburban family. "But it appeared that we were as close to it as we could be."

"I think we are all very good at hiding the reality of our lives," she says. "But I don't hesitate to talk about this, because I don't want people to get the impression that, just because you look like you've got it all together, you do."

From the beginning, Fran recalls, Alice, their eldest, was "a good kid and a great daughter." No star student, she was "not college-bound" but academically okay. "Socially, she didn't hang out with anybody that concerned us. We never had problems with her breaking curfew, trying to sneak out, or going places she shouldn't—at least never that we were aware of."

Those last words bring a hint of darkness into Fran's voice. "I guess I was a little naive," she admits. "Our level of trust in her had been built up to a point that, if there were warning signs, we completely missed them."

The problems began when Alice, after graduating from high school at age eighteen, moved into an apartment with a girlfriend. For a while, all went well. "She had a good job, and she seemed to be well respected," Fran remembers. The roommate, however, turned out to be "a dud," and Alice moved back home, which is where she was living when she announced her pregnancy.

"I was completely surprised," says Fran, "but we stood by her. We all valued life, and we told her that we would help to do whatever she chose to do in deciding whether to keep the baby or seek adoption." Although the baby's father was "in denial"—there was never any question of marriage or a more stable partnership— Alice insisted on keeping her child. So baby Tina became part of Fran's household.

For a while, that arrangement worked. Alice found work, and Fran and her husband shared the babysitting duties, always making it clear to Tina that her mother was the decision maker and that they were only grandparents. But when Tina was in first grade, Alice decided to move in with a man she'd been seeing, taking Tina with her. She became pregnant again, but after eighteen months broke off that relationship and returned home again, now with two children.

Although Alice continued working, Fran and her husband noticed a change. "There was a lot more napping and sleeping and surrendering of the parenting role to us," Fran says. The reason? "She had experienced some medical problems that we were not aware of and had gotten hooked on prescription painkillers."

Still, they soldiered on. With her children now seven and two and a half years old, Alice would come home from work, have dinner, do homework with the kids, put them to bed, and head for bed herself. Fran thought all was well until one night when, awakening at 4:30 A.M., she met her daughter returning home from a night out. Alice, who was working at a TGI Friday's restaurant, had gotten into the habit of sneaking out of the house at about

11:00 P.M. to party with friends from the restaurant after they got off work.

"She knew we were there," says Fran, so "in her mind she wasn't abandoning" the children. Still, it came as a shock to the grand-parents—and put them increasingly in charge of the little girls. Whenever they addressed such behavior with Alice, she was contrite and apologetic, vowing to change her ways. But it was becoming clear that the drug use was growing. In fact, it was Tina who tipped them off. Having learned from her drug education classes at school what signs to look for, she told her grandparents that Alice was smoking crack cocaine.

In the confrontation that followed, says Fran, "We told her in no uncertain terms that the behavior had to stop, and that there was no way we could allow her to use drugs in the house—because if *she* gets arrested, *we* get arrested, and that's not happening!"

Despite all the apologies, however, the problem snowballed. Alice began getting sick and missing work, and she eventually lost her job. Yet she refused to consider drug rehabilitation treatments. That's when, as Fran puts it, "you find people who will supply your drug needs for whatever reason"—people who, in this case, were living in "a part of town that I wouldn't want to *drive* through, let alone go and visit."

And so came the first severe hurdle for Fran and her husband: whether to take legal custody of the girls, whom they had raised almost as their own children and to whom they were extremely close. They had already begun the process when, on a Fourth of July weekend, Alice left the children with her parents to "visit a friend" on Sunday afternoon.

"By Wednesday morning," Fran recalls, "we still didn't know where she was—no contact, no answering the phone or anything." When she finally turned up, it was clear that temporary custody was the best course. Alice agreed, the judge approved, and she moved out, leaving her children behind.

"She came back once," Fran says. "We did the old prodigal son kind of thing. My husband and I said, 'How can we not do this?' So we let her come back."

About four weeks after that, they discovered prescription painkillers in the house, along with evidence of crack. At that point, with all that had been building up over the years, Fran and her husband faced a stark choice between their daughter and their grandchildren. Should they banish Alice from the only home she had in order to protect their grandchildren from their mother's influence? Or should they continue trying to nurture and sustain their daughter at the risk of harming Tina, now nine years old, and her sister?

Telling me her story, Fran puts her dilemma crisply into focus. "I'll always believe that the role of a parent is to do whatever they can to provide for their children," she says, "and part of providing for [our daughter] was providing a home, and taking care of her needs, and helping her do whatever she needed to do. On the other hand, Tina was nine, and except for about a two-and-a-half-year period, she had lived with us her whole life. Tina was practically my fifth child."

Standing for Conscience When Both Sides Are Right

What are the tensions Fran faced in this choice? A quick scan suggests that all of our four paradigms are in play. Loyalty to Alice is present in numerous ways—yet it always comes squarely up against the truth of what Alice's example may do to her daughters. Alice's enormous needs as an individual are present as well, though they run directly counter to the needs of the family group for harmony and consistency. With crack cocaine in play, justice would require law enforcement to sweep in—while mercy, knowing the underlying goodness of a young woman who was once "a good kid and a great daughter," seeks reformation through softer channels. Finally, Fran and her husband could easily conclude that what's right in the short term is to take a nonconfrontational week-by-week approach—although by doing so, they took the risk that some sudden turn of events could produce a catastrophic long-term result. Or they could opt for the long-term security of the grandchildren—at the cost of an immediate, severe, and perhaps irreversible severing of their relationship with their daughter.

What did they do? "We told her she had to leave," says Fran. "We packed her bags and took her where she wanted us to take her—and that was that."

How do they explain that choice? Fran recalls that "it got to the point that, regardless of how much it was hurtful, my responsibility to those children who had no advocate but us was to be that advocate—even if it meant doing what we had to do with our own child, which was really kind of saying, 'Go away!' "

Tucked into Fran's rationale are overtones of each of our three resolution principles:

- *Ends based.* Implicit in Fran's comments is a focus on the consequences, the outcomes, the results. Doing "the greatest good for the greatest number," after all, means finding those end states that harm the fewest people and sustain the most. The reason her grandchildren needed an advocate was that the consequences they faced weren't hypothetical but real: there was crack in the house. Only by taking the children's side, Fran felt, could they be protected from those threats.

- *Rule based.* Yet Fran is also thinking like a Kantian. The universal law—the guiding precept she would want everyone to adopt in similar circumstances—was for her a rule that involved responsibility. Her duty was to demand responsibility from her daughter—and to enforce that demand unbendingly, even if the consequences were heartbreaking. It's as though she had to choose whether to live in a world where everyone always insists on responsibility or one where everyone always gave others another chance—a complicated and difficult choice for the best of parents. Insisting on responsibility, she let the chips fall where they would—even if it meant saying, "Go away!" to her daughter.

- *Care based.* But what if Fran puts herself in Alice's shoes? What would she want her own mother to do to her? Alice herself seems confused on this point, wanting her mother to let her come back but refusing to go into rehab or break away from her group. Fran seems to be looking right through Alice and seeing the children themselves as the "others." Would they want Grandma to let Mommy use crack? Or would they want to be protected from that situation?

In this circumstance, all three of the resolution principles appear to point to the same decision: send the daughter away. And that's unusual. In our seminars, as we watch individuals struggle with their dilemmas, they often find that ends-based logic supports one side, while rule-based reasoning supports the other and the care-based arguments can support both. Here there's no divergence: every way Fran turns, it seems, the decision is clear.

Clear, yes, but not easy. "I never thought it was going to be this hard to be a parent," she told me. Think how much less courage it would take for her to say, "We'll let you stay just a little longer." Instead, Fran and her husband exhibited moral courage, which we've defined as the willing endurance of significant risk for the sake of principle. They acted for the sake of a principle that involved responsibility and the care of their grandchildren. They endured the moment of crisis as they packed their daughter's bags and drove her away. They faced the very real risk of a possible loss of any relationship with their daughter, as well as the loss of her stability, health, and perhaps even life. But did Fran and her husband allow the issue to reach this stage solely because they were too naive, too trusting? No. Trust doesn't mean that you examine every possible outcome and take only the most carefully calculated risks. "Trusting is taking not-so-calculated risks," writes the feminist moral philosopher Annette C. Baier, "which are not the same as ill-judged ones. Part of what it is to trust is not to have too many thoughts about possible betrayals. They would turn trust into mistrust."[4]

Making Tough Choices Even When You Doubt Yourself

There's more to the story. In the ensuing years, Tina prospered in school. Her mother, meanwhile, got entangled with a group forging checks and stealing credit card data at casinos to support their drug habits, and eventually she spent seven years in prison. Fran stayed in touch as best she could, and from time to time Alice pleaded with her to be allowed to return home.

"Will you check into a treatment program?" Fran would ask her.

"Oh, I can't do that."

"Will you not be around those people?"

"Oh, I can't do that—they really care about me."

It was, as Fran recalled, "a very torturous period of time."

Finally, as Tina was applying for college, there seemed to be a breakthrough. It was becoming clear that Tina's "temporary custody" had to be made permanent. Colleges were growing wary of students from well-off homes claiming to live with grandparents of modest means—and therefore seeming to be eligible for increased scholarship funds. While that clearly wasn't Tina's case, the word *temporary* seemed to be a red flag in college admissions circles. When Fran explained that point to Alice, she agreed to allow the change.

"Mom, I will always be their mother," Fran recalls her saying, "but I know that they will never be with me again. You do whatever you need to do to make things okay for Tina."

"I believe it was said in all sincerity," Fran says, "and it's one of the first honest, genuine signs of hope that I've had in a long time. Maybe this thirty-six-year-old woman is finally an adult."

Fran's story wraps together many of the themes of this book. She found herself facing a right-versus-right dilemma because of someone else's right-versus-wrong temptations. She encountered, in Diana Baumrind's terms, the tension between permissive and authoritarian parenting (discussed in Chapter Three)—and worried that she allowed Alice to "get to the point where she knew what we wanted to hear" and didn't push back when that was all she told them. And clearly she was forced to express moral courage in taking her stand and having the tough conversations that, as she says, "have to be had." Her story also reminds us that parenting is never finished. As a crusty Jason Robards puts it in the movie *Parenthood* (1989), "There's no goal line in parenting, no end zone where you spike the ball and that's it."

Yet through it all, Fran has made her peace with a question that nibbles at the mental edges of so many parents interviewed for this book: *Am I a good parent?* "I used to think, 'Oh, obviously, I'm a terrible mother, because look how my child turned out!'" Fran says. She finds some solace in the fact that Alice's three siblings have turned out well and are deeply upset with Alice for what she has done to them, her parents, and her own children. In Alice's case, she says, "There were so many other factors completely out of my control. I think parents bear a great responsibility. But I don't think they should ever feel guilty—that somehow it's *my* fault, not *her* fault."

"Part of ethical thinking," she concludes, "is to help our children understand their responsibility—and to help parents see that our job is to do just that."

Supporting Your Daughter or Saving Your Grandchildren

- Even in the toughest moral choices—like deciding between the needs of your child and the safety of your grandchildren—applying the lenses in this book brings clarity.
- Parents may miss warning signs, but that doesn't mean they're naive or too trusting. Trust is essential in parenting and can stand you in good stead no matter how old your children are.
- If a showdown comes, moral courage needs to be steady, consistent, and unwavering. Holding to a right principle is a long-term commitment.
- Guilt doesn't help. Raising three other great kids and two grandchildren is a reminder that good parenting is doing your best to help others be responsible.

The Difference Between Courage and Stubbornness

Sometimes, as in Fran's case, a dilemma can seem to build up for years and to take equally long to unwind into its final disposition. Yet however long the before-and-after process may be, the point of decision, when it comes, is typically quick and pointed. Fran didn't say how much time elapsed between finding the drug paraphernalia and ushering Alice out the door for the last time, but it can't have been long.

For Amanda, too, the decision point arrived suddenly and forcefully—though here, too, the issue had been coming to a head for several years. As a full-time working mother, Amanda is committed to raising three children—one of her own and two brought to her marriage by her second husband. She sees her situation as uncomfortably commonplace. "This world is so divided," she says, that "not too many people are married anymore that had children together—mostly it is stepparents and stepchildren."

More Statistics on Divorce

Census figures support Amanda's perception. In 1990—the last figures available before the U.S. Census Bureau stopped providing estimates of marriage, divorce, and remarriage—the data showed that:

- More than half of all first marriages end in divorce

- Forty-three percent of all marriages are remarriages for at least one adult

- Nearly two-thirds of remarriages involve children from prior marriages[5]

Based on those data, the Census Bureau estimated that by 2000, there would be more stepfamilies than original families in the United States.[6]

Given this situation, says Amanda, the first thing that parents need to do if they are stepparents is to "take the *step* out of it." Speaking from her own experience, she insists, "There is no *step*. Either you're a parent or you're not."

For Amanda, parenting has always been about core values, especially honesty. In her home, ethics has typically been understood as a collection of fixed rules and standards, moderated by the guidance of intuition. She wants her children to let their hearts be their guide. "If it feels *right*—not *good*, there's a difference—if it feels right, it probably is," she tells them. "If it feels wrong, it's not right. And if you're ever questioning it, it's not ready, it's not the time."

These standards came from her own mother, who imparted the simplest of principles. "She always said, 'Just be honest,'" Amanda recalls, "and I never wanted to let her down"—especially, she adds, because "I had two siblings who were rotten to the core."

The Cloud of Abuse

Her parents got divorced so early that Amanda can't remember her father. The reason was that he was physically and mentally abusive. Knowing that background, she has been especially alert to signs of abusiveness in her own life. "I recognized that I could be abusive—not physically, but probably verbally, I could be very demanding," she says. "There's a line where you have to be careful, because when you start demanding things it can get abusive. You have to really watch yourself. When you have those tendencies—I think you're born with them, and I think you've got to recognize it right off the bat so that you can fix it, because if you don't recognize it you're not going to fix it."

Whether she was "born" with abusive tendencies or led to them by being abused herself is a question psychophysiologists and neuroscientists can debate. Studies of children abused by their parents suggest that compared to nonabused children, they develop different patterns of face recognition—an area long of interest to neurobiologists. "The importance of the many signals [a face] conveys (e.g., emotion, identity, direction of eye gaze), together with the speed and ease with which adults typically process this information, are compelling reasons to suppose that there may exist brain circuits specialized for processing faces," write Charles A. Nelson and his colleagues in an extensive review of brain research on cognitive development.[7] Abused children, it appears, are much quicker to detect signs of anger than other children. The perception of "the facial expression of anger, but not other expressions," they write, "is altered in children who are abused by their parents."[8]

While that finding might confirm Amanda's suspicion about herself—that her background has altered her—it could give her some solace about her biological son, Evan. If, after all, responses to abuse are learned rather than innate, there may be no genetic propensity toward abuse that could affect her son, since he was never abused. Nevertheless, she says, "I've told my son, 'Be careful. You are persistent, so you want to make sure you don't have any tendencies of being abusive. You never want to be that way.'"

For whatever reason, she now finds herself with "a real big conscience—huge." If she's done something wrong in her life, she feels an overwhelming need to fix it. On one occasion, she recalls, shortly after her own early divorce, she discovered that she was dating a married man she thought was also divorced. "He lived here, he didn't wear a ring," she says, "and then I found out that he was only separated."

"I went right to his wife and I told her," she says. "I didn't even know her. She could have shot me. But it didn't matter, because it was right. You always know the right thing. I dumped him, and went to her, and told her, and she and I are friends to this day. That was seventeen years ago."

You always know the right thing. That assurance of moral clarity has stood like a beacon in Amanda's life from her earliest days. So when Evan, at age nineteen, got in trouble over his car payments, she found herself in a particularly wrenching position. Facing a dilemma that took her well beyond any right-versus-wrong formula, she discovered that "the right thing" turned out to characterize both sides of her conundrum.

Evan, she admits with a chuckle, is "the most stubborn child you have ever met—how I got him raised without killing him, I just don't know." She also notes, with some understatement, that he and his stepbrother "weren't overachievers" at school. "They were like, 'Let's get through this, because school is not my thing. Now put me with an engine and let me use my hands, and we'll get somewhere—just get me away from these books!'"

Sticking to a Contract with Your Child

When Amanda and I spoke one snowy December afternoon, Evan was only months away from finishing high school. He could have graduated the prior June, she said, but he chose to take another semester to finish up a couple of courses. So that fall he attended school every other day, using his car to leave right after his last class.

When he bought the car earlier in that year, Amanda had loaned him five thousand dollars, with a note under which he agreed to pay her one hundred dollars each month. He and she agreed to the terms at the outset: if he misses a payment, the car gets parked until he cleans up his account. All went well for the first few months. But over the summer, Evan and his girlfriend became, in her words, "more intimate." Amanda has always drawn a firm line about sexual matters: "If you live in my home—I don't care if you're twenty-five—you're not spending the night with your girlfriend," she says. "If you want to do that, then that means you're old enough to get out and get a job and get an apartment."

But so adamant was Evan that when his girlfriend's mother was planning to be away from home late in the summer, he decided to move in with her for a week—and to quit his job to have more time with her. The tension was explosive, and Amanda endured "countless nights of no sleep"—though, as she freely admits, "I love him more than life itself."

She and Evan eventually patched up that problem, and he moved back home. But with the economy in difficulty, he found it hard to get another job. He managed to land some temporary work with both his biological father and his stepfather, Amanda's husband, which kept the car payments current through November. But then came December—and now, says Amanda, "the clock is ticking to January 1st with no car payment."

"So he comes to me and he says, 'I'm really stressed about you taking my car.' And I said, 'It's the eleventh hour. I know you are. Sorry.'"

"Can I have two more weeks to find a job?"

"No."

"Why?"

"Because," Amanda told him, "you've had two months. It wasn't important to you then. You won't understand without the pain. If you don't have a car payment to me by January 1st, you don't have a car. If you don't have a job between January 1st and February 1st, the car goes on the market for sale. And if the car goes on the market for sale, Mom never does this for you again. We were very clear, Evan. You knew the guidelines; you accepted them fully. And I'm not going to waver from them."

Amanda told me that she knew, as she took this stand, that his rejoinder could well be to tell her that he "just might not graduate," because he refused to ride the school bus. If he did that, she said, she would have to stick to her position and say, "'Okay, that's your deal.' I set rules. I have to go by them. I'm not going to waver. If he quits, he quits—it's up to him." But that, she admits, is "the hardest part of being a parent. It's saying, 'Wow, it *is* his deal.' He just might quit if I don't give him this car. But he just might call my bluff if I do."

What Amanda has just articulated, in the sharpest possible terms, is a right-versus-right dilemma that richly expresses all four of the dilemma paradigms:

- *Truth versus loyalty.* The arguments for loyalty are potent. This is her son, whom she loves "more than life itself." Her duty is to support him in every possible situation, whether the threat is external (a difficult economy) or internal (his lack of wisdom). Yet the truth staring her in the face is that without some kind of correction, he'll keep muddling along, putting wants before needs and perhaps abandoning his education simply to spite her.

- *Short term versus long term.* If she honors the needs of the short term, she relents and lets him keep his car even without a job—though that course of action risks compounding his irresponsibility in the future. If, however, she honors the long term, she holds her ground and forces him to face up to his mistakes— even though the immediate result could be the termination of his education and another rift with her.

- *Individual versus community.* Thinking of Evan as the individual in this dilemma, she clearly sees the need for delivering a character-building lesson by stripping away the car. But the consequences of that choice on the community of her family could be severe, forcing them to endure the logistical complexity of ferrying him between school and work and even risking an explosion during which he storms out of school and disappears from their lives.

- *Justice versus mercy.* The demands of justice are obvious: Evan made a solemn promise that must be obeyed, and there are well-understood and agreed-on penalties for breaking that promise. But the demands of mercy are equally salient: here's a situation where forgiveness, absolving him of his self-imposed difficulties, could tide him over into a brighter future, softening a punishment that perhaps doesn't fit the crime.

Applying the Principles of Resolution

How is she to decide? Here she has access to one or more of the resolution principles. If she argues for an ends-based principle, she'll examine the consequences, weigh the risks of various outcomes, and probably determine that the greatest good for Evan, his family, and the community of which he is a part would be for him to finish school without the added hardship of worrying about his car. But this principle could also take her in the opposite direction: she could reason that the greatest good for the community would be to compel Evan to take charge of his responsibilities, honor his promises, and exhibit the moral courage to swallow his pride, ride the bus, and complete his education—and that only a severe jolt to his system would create the kind of citizen that the community truly needs. Ends-based reasoning, then, could carry her either way.

As a rule-based thinker, Amanda would find it natural to search for an overarching principle. What she wants to find is, in the words of Emmanuel Kant, the "maxim" that "should become a universal law." Since maxims typically begin with "always" or "never," Amanda needs to find some principle, precept, or rule that she would like to see guide not only Evan but everyone like him for the rest of their lives—causing them always to do certain things and never to do others. If the maxim is, "Always honor promises," then Amanda must take away his car. But if the maxim is, "Always forgive"—or even "Always pursue your education"—then she must relent. Here the moral challenge becomes supreme indeed. Faced with a choice of having to live in a world where everyone always kept promises or one in which everyone always forgave mistakes, which would you want? Tough choice. Here, too, rule-based thinking could carry her in either direction.

Finally, she can turn to the care-based principle of the Golden Rule. If she were Evan, what would she want a parent to do to her? The immediate answer, of course, goes something like this: "Relax, Mom, and give me break! Can't you see this is tough? I know I sort of blew it. But I need your help to get through." With that logic, she'd let him keep the car. But the Golden Rule speaks of doing to *others* what we'd want them to do to us—and there are other "others" here. In this story, however, their interests may well be aligned with Evan's. The school principal, Evan's teachers, his classmates—they'd all want him to stay in school. Even her own family, foreseeing the tension that might arise if she grounded him, might urge her to relent. And there's yet another character to consider: Evan-in-the-future. Will this admittedly fictional character look back, years from now, and thank his mom for holding firm?

Whichever choice Amanda makes will be ethical, but one side will take more moral courage than the other. Relenting is easy: Evan finishes school, and peace reigns in the family. Holding firm is tough: tears may flow, tempers may rise, and a parent-child relationship may be put at risk forever.

What, then, did Amanda do?

Sticking to her position but recognizing that the economy was tough, she kept insisting that Evan make an effort to set up some job interviews. On the Friday of the week when the car payment was due, she phoned him to ask whether he had any interviews scheduled for the weekend. He didn't. So she laid down the law: the car gets parked at the house for the weekend.

"Then I'm quitting school," he said. "I can't believe you're doing this to me!"

Her rejoinder was equally firm, offering him two choices: either he meets her that day at 3:45 when she finishes with her last customer, or he calls the school principal and schedules an exit interview. If he does the latter, she has directions for him: "You head on home, leave the car, go in the house, pack your bags, and start walking. You will not live in my house and be unproductive!"

It was a moment of truth for both of them. He could tell by her voice, she says, that something had happened. "I think he pushed me to a limit," she says, adding that she "was way past the anger stage"—so much so that she used the F word with him, something she had never done. "But I got really tired of the give-and-take. I recognized that I *just had to be done with it!*"

The result? He was there at 3:45. They talked it through, and he agreed to stay in school. For her part, she agreed to let him use the car to get to school and to go to job interviews. She insisted they put it all down in writing. "We have a contract," she says, requiring that if he gets "anything below an 80" in his grades, the car gets parked again.

It may be years before she knows the real end of the story. When we last talked, he had a 92 average in school—and five job interviews. He'd been accepted at a local community college, pending a successful graduation. And she had let him in on a secret: she'd been saving up his car payments, she told him, and was planning to give them back to him, with the car, as a present when he graduated.

Amanda's story is one of moral courage, which in its simplest definition is the courage to be moral. She knew she had to take a stand for the core values of responsibility, honesty, and fairness. She was lucidly aware of the risks. "I'm not being a witch about it," she told him—though she might well have wondered, in the quiet reaches of the night, whether in fact she was. While she had reason to fear that he might run off the rails and perhaps become, like her own siblings, "rotten to the core," she also had reason to fear that her own stand was abusive and overblown—that perhaps she *was* being a witch. Yet she had the courage to put down her fears and move forward.

And that's a key point about moral courage: it's not the same as fearlessness. Amanda had the strength of character to meet the challenge and hold her ground. Does that mean that every parent, facing a situation like this, should do the same? No. This is, after all, a right-versus-right situation, where both sides have powerful moral arguments in their favor. Good parents could certainly choose the other course. But isn't it always right for parents to choose the side that takes the most courage? No again. There are times when it will be right to let mercy trump justice and when the easier way *is* the right way. Notice how Amanda did it. In the end, she found a trilemma option. Her third way through the dilemma involved small but important concessions—like allowing Evan to use the car for school rather than taking the bus. A witch might not have done that. Amanda did.

And was the game worth the candle? Did all her effort accomplish its purpose?

"I feel like we were very successful," she says, reflecting on the entire experience. "I think it was a turning point in his life, too. There was a huge wake-up call."

Lessons from

The Difference Between Courage and Stubbornness

- Standing for conscience—our third lens—can sometimes appear harsh, even abusive. But the former is unselfish, while the latter is about ego and domination.
- When young adults are plunged into newly found independence, they may see it as a license to abandon responsibility. Parents can remind them of moral obligations.
- Children, even as young adults, test limits—and pluck at heart strings. Sometimes parents need to give, and sometimes they need to stand firm—and either side can be right.
- Trilemmas can save the day. Keeping her contract but relaxing some rules, Amanda let her son stay in school. And the result—getting good grades and applying for college—was sweet indeed.

7

Conclusion

At sixteen, Deming was moody, melancholic, monosyllabic—and hopelessly in love. The buoyancy and charm of early adolescence, when he had chuckled his way through the toughest classes at school and emerged with top grades, had given way to an inwardness that, if not exactly surly, was notably distant and reserved. He still had friends with whom he chatted at length and texted incessantly. But the calls, at least when his parents were around, were carried on in whispers, grunts, and sighs—and the answers to his messages seemed only to make him less responsive.

His parents, Jim and Elaine, read the barometer of his bleakness as an indicator of his relationship with Candy. They didn't know Candy well, but what they saw gave them pause. On the occasions when Elaine, a warmhearted stay-at-home mom, and Jim, a fast-rising executive of an Oklahoma mineral company, had dinner with Deming and Candy, she seemed consumed with herself—a bit too pushy and controlling, they thought, and too quick to take offense and belittle Deming. Yet Deming seemed to notice little beyond her drop-dead good looks, her captivating smile, and the flightiness of her nearly nonstop conversation.

For a while, Jim was inclined to shrug it off. He saw in his son a reflection of his own youth—his rhapsody in the presence of his sweetheart, his listlessness in her absence, his self-flagellating reex-amination of their every conversation to discover what a fool he had made of himself. The more Jim and Elaine observed Deming, the more they noticed a deeper darkness, a more serious and sustained depression. Were his oblique references to death just an adolescent fascination with the macabre, no more important than a taste for horror movies or a penchant for the supernatural? Or did they hint at a suicidal tendency? They decided to keep a closer watch and agreed that one of them should always be nearby when he was home from school on afternoons, evenings, and weekends.

As the year wore on, there seemed no letup in Deming's depression. Finally, in the run-up to the junior-senior prom, he received a devastating blow. He and Candy had long had plans to attend, as everyone at school assumed they would. But suddenly, in a fit of annoyance, she announced that she was going with someone else—not someone from school, but a young man from Florida she'd met at a summer camp who was flying in for the weekend. For Jim, it was time for some executive decision making. He told his company he'd be taking a break—two days, a week, he wasn't sure. Then, with Elaine's full blessing, he packed up his new pickup, gathered up Deming, and headed west. They didn't have a plan— they were just striking out, father and son, with no more purpose than to be together.

For the first day, Jim recalls, it was agonizing. Deming wasn't rebellious and seemed in his own way to appreciate his father's attention. But he said little, and Jim knew he couldn't pry. He had to let the conversation find its own level. But the next day, the discussion turned to the prom and Deming's devastation at Candy's rejection. In an effort to console him, Jim asked whether he could go with someone else—at which Deming shot him a look of incredulity, as though he'd come from Mars. But Jim persisted. Wasn't there *anyone* else Deming liked being with? What about Kimball?

A longtime neighborhood friend, Kimball was fun loving and zany, and with a good-hearted affection for humanity and a natural independence. She had little in the way of a home life; her parents had all but abandoned her. But she was hard working and smart. Having finished high school at midyear, she was now working as a waitress and putting herself through college. Jim had always kind of liked her—not least for the time when, several years earlier, he'd had to control his laughter and deliver a stern rebuke to them both when he caught them on the back porch smoking cigars she'd smuggled out of her father's desk. But Jim also knew he had to play his hand carefully and stick to his driving, lest he push too hard and cause Deming to dig in his heels and lapse back into darkness.

In a few more miles, however, and without much more conversation, Deming took out his cell phone. When Kimball answered, and he asked her whether she'd go to the prom with him, Jim could hear her screech of delight. He also heard her say she didn't have a dress. "I'll buy her one!" Jim heard himself silently mouthing, before he realized that that would have overstepped some indescribable but certain line. But just as quickly, he heard Kimball say she knew where she could borrow one. In a few minutes, when Deming hung up, he seemed like a new person. The next seven hours, as they rolled west toward Big Bend, Deming was almost, Jim reflected, his former self. The road trip seemed to be working, and Jim was delighted.

And then Deming's phone rang. Jim's heart sank as his son answered, paused, and then said, "Hi, Candy." For a while, Jim sensed, it was just chitchat. Then she must have asked him what he was going to do about the prom.

"I've got a date," he said, without telling her who.

Candy's voice rose to where Jim could hear her say, "You can't do that to me!" And then, to his horror, she announced that she was breaking her date with the Florida friend and wanted Deming to go with her.

Jim couldn't stare—he was driving, after all. In a sideways glance he noticed that as Deming sat and listened, tears were streaming down his face. At that point, he recalls, it was all he could do not to intervene—stop the truck, take charge of the situation as an executive would, and tell Deming what he had to do. Instead he just gripped the wheel and kept going.

Then he heard something that made him glance over again in astonishment. "No," said Deming, "I can't do that." The tears were still streaming, but Deming's voice was oddly controlled and clear. More silence, more indecipherable noise from the other end of the phone. "Because I promised, that's why. I can't do that to her." More noise, more passion, more tears. Then a final, "I just can't."

He hung up, and the cab was filled with nothing but the high-speed sound of the road. Outwardly Jim was just driving—though inwardly he was crying out, "That's my boy!!" After a while, Deming turned to him.

"She's not a very nice person," he stated.

Inwardly, Jim shouted out his agreement; outwardly, he held his peace.

"She already broke her promise to me, and now she wants to break her promise to this other guy—and wants me to break my promise as well! She's really not very nice."

It wasn't until they were at the motel that night—staying, as they always did, in the same room so Jim could be properly watchful—that Jim had a chance to call Elaine while Deming was in the shower. He could hardly contain himself: he was as proud of his son as he'd ever been, he told her, and he felt they'd reached a real turning point.

And so it proved to be. Deming and Kimball went to the prom—good friends, as ever, but with no romantic attachment. Some years later, Deming married and had children. He recently told his dad that Candy, now divorced, had suddenly called him, fishing around for a relationship. He had no difficulty putting her off. Jim, reflecting on the situation, told me he felt that she'd probably keep trying to cycle back and snag him for the rest of his life. "She really is *evil*," he told me with a chuckle.

After all he's been through, why can he chuckle? Because in the space of a few hours in that new pickup truck, he watched as all three of the lenses came together in a crisp, lasting moment of truth. All along, it seems, Deming had a sense for the first lens, knowing what's right. Whipsawed by his emotions, he bounced between hope and despair in his relationship with Candy. But when it came to making tough choices (lens 2), he held firmly to his core values (lens 1) and found himself standing for conscience (lens 3). For Jim, too, the lenses came into play, especially the third. His hardest task, he told me, was in refusing to force the conversation and instead letting Deming speak up when he wanted to, refusing to bustle in with an offer to buy Kimball a dress, waiting patiently to hear Deming tell him about Candy's promise breaking and lack of responsibility, holding his breath when he wanted to cheer like a football fan. All that takes moral courage.

But perhaps the greater courage came from his sudden, emphatic decision to break away from work and drive off into the sunset with his son for a few days. Had he not done so, who could have blamed him? But something told him this was the moment, the time his son needed him most. This was no time for blame. He knew that Deming, despite his moodiness, was essentially a good kid facing a tough choice. He also knew this had to be a father-son moment, where his full attention could be devoted to Deming. Yet he also knew he couldn't let his attention turn into smothering, his conversation descend into hectoring, his affection morph into emotion.

How Emotion and Morality Interact

Jim's story illustrates how parents, facing the emotions that arise during moral choices, can provide stability and ballast. A friend of mine once called it "the level-eyebrow approach." By that, he didn't mean a stony, aloof appearance—a kind of Mt. Rushmore parenting style. He was talking about the need to listen carefully without letting the jarring disclosures of a conversation show on

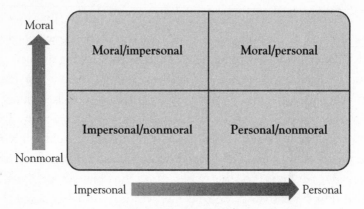

Figure 7.1   Four Flavors of Dilemmas

your face. Jim, of course, had an easy out: he was driving, after all, and had to keep his eyebrows facing the road. But that didn't mean he was insulated from the emotions arising from his son's dilemma.

Some dilemmas, however, raise much stronger emotions than others. Dilemmas, in fact, seem to come in four flavors, illustrated in Figure 7.1. Those flavors are based on two things: whether the dilemmas raise moral issues and whether they are personal or impersonal. According to some early neurobiological research, it appears that only one flavor—those that are both personal and moral—can evoke strong emotions. First, though, let's look at the other kinds.

The simplest dilemmas, in the lower-left quadrant, are both impersonal and nonmoral. Should the nation fund big-ticket science projects like the superconducting supercollider, or invest in thousands of smaller projects with breakthrough potential? Should a successful restaurant with a gallery theme move across the street to a larger but less artsy space? Should the city continue picking up the trash with its own employees and trucks, or bid out the contract to private firms? Such issues require plenty of analysis and sound argumentation on both sides. But they are neither inherently about moral choices nor (for most people) intensely personal matters. Like many other policy or business decisions, these choices simply present a logical debate between two valid opinions.

The dilemmas in the lower right of Figure 7.1 are still non-moral, though these are quite personal. Do I walk the dog this afternoon in the rain, or wait until dark when it's harder to see but might be dry? Do I drive home from work the shorter way with many more stoplights, or swing around on the interstate? Will the family spend the afternoon bicycling or attending the local fair? These are undoubtedly personal matters, but it's hard to find any strong moral content in the choices. Pushed to extremes, of course, the dilemmas in these bottom two quadrants might raise moral issues. If you thought, for example, that your dog hated rain or that big science was corrupted by big bribes, you might find yourself facing a moral choice. At their core, however, these dilemmas have no notable moral content.

Other dilemmas, however, can be deeply moral but (for us, at least) essentially impersonal—the upper-left quadrant. Should President Harry S. Truman have dropped the atomic bomb on Japan to end World War II, or invaded from the sea at huge cost to American forces? Should northern communities use salt to melt ice on the frozen highways and risk groundwater pollution, or should they simply spread sand and let drivers do their best on slick surfaces? Should cities send police units to help an earthquake-ravaged country, or continue protecting their own neighborhoods from rising levels of crime during a recession? Such dilemmas bring powerful moral arguments into play—although unless you have a role like that of a truck driver in the second example or a crime-plagued home owner in the third, the impact remains essentially impersonal.

Finally, there are dilemmas that are deeply moral *and* intensely personal, such as the one Deming faced. These dilemmas, residing in the upper-right-hand moral/personal quadrant of the figure, fully engage the emotions and have the most potential for affecting our judgments.

In a study published in *Science* in 2001, a team of neurobiology researchers at Princeton University and the University of Pittsburgh led by Joshua D. Greene found that moral-personal dilemmas tended to create "salient, automatic" responses that activate parts of the brain normally associated with emotional expression.[1] The data, they write, "strongly [suggest] that the increased emotional responses generated by the moral-personal dilemmas have an influence on and are not merely incidental to moral judgment."[2] Their point is that when a deeply personal situation raises serious moral issues, the resulting emotions don't merely arise in parallel with our decision-making process. Nor is the emotion a by-product of our choice. Instead, the emotion may have a direct effect on the way we come to judgment. This may seem a complex explanation for an age-old adage—*Don't let your emotions color your judgment!* But it does serve to remind us to be particularly alert when making tough decisions about issues that are both moral and personal.

The research also reminds us that how we come to judgment may depend more on whether the dilemma is personal than whether it is moral. "Judgments concerning 'impersonal' dilemmas," write Greene and his colleagues, "more closely resemble judgments concerning non-moral dilemmas than they do judgments concerning 'personal' moral dilemmas."[3] In other words, how I respond when the issue is impersonal—the two boxes in the left-hand column of our diagram—is closely aligned to how I respond when a dilemma, even though personal, has little moral content. Dilemmas that blend the personal and the moral issues, by contrast, cause us to operate in a different realm.

Why is that distinction so important? Because by their very nature, the moral dilemmas of parenting are always personal— tightly bound up with family, involving people we know well and care for deeply. In Jim's relationship to Deming, for example, the intensity of the experience came from the fact that Deming was his own son. Had Jim been driving west with a relative stranger—one of his firm's employees, for instance, or a farmhand who needed a ride to Texas—their conversation could well have raised issues laden with moral content. And while Jim's interests and sympathies as a caring human being could have been greatly engaged—and while, like a professional counselor, he could have found many ways to be helpful—the personal and emotional connection might not have been so readily aroused. But parenting, by definition, isn't impersonal. As we recognize that fact, we're better able to foresee the emotions that may arise in our children and in ourselves when moral questions arise. Knowing that, we can make special efforts to bring the conversation back to the three lenses. That doesn't mean we need to talk specifically about those lenses. We simply need to be alert to their presence as shaping forces in our ethical lives.

Using the Moral Toolkit

How do you cultivate that alertness? Through steady practice. As you work with these lenses, you'll find you're better able to address ethical issues—even the ones that raise the most emotional issues—if you keep a moral toolkit at the ready. Three tools are particularly useful for parents: an enhanced awareness of moral issues, a set of entry points for generating discussions with children, and a commitment to results. Here's how they can be used:

------

1. *Moral awareness.* With this toolkit, you can use the three lenses to spot ethical issues as they arise on the horizon. Too often parents facing a tough situation blast right past the most important first questions: Why is this tough? What are the complex elements here? Why do I feel such tension? Without sufficient moral awareness, you may think the issues your kids are facing are merely about

disobedience, lack of sleep, a poor diet, or too much TV. Or you may think they're only about fashion, athletics, economics, or poor work habits. Each of these may trigger challenges you need to address. But with remarkable frequency, the question behind the question turns out to be about honesty, respect, responsibility, fairness, and compassion—in other words, about the application of values to decision making. Only when you're alert to the values-based issues at play in your children's lives will you see any role for ethical analysis and resolution in addressing them.

2. *Entry points for discussion.* This tool reminds us that we can use our lenses to give us multiple ways into any issue. Facing tough situations with your children, you may find yourself desperately wanting to engage. *But how,* you may ask, *do I start the conversation?* The answer is to take it back to basics. Is there a discussion needed here about fairness, or honesty, or respect? Is it about irresponsibility? Does it suggest a lack of compassion? Does this situation call for a conversation about the right-versus-right paradigms: truth versus loyalty, perhaps, or to put it another way, about candor versus allegiance or transparency versus fidelity? Can we talk about personal needs against the best interests of the group, or about what's best immediately as opposed to what's good for the long haul, or about an expectation of justice versus a merciful exception? Should we be discussing differing views on how to resolve ethical dilemmas—doing the most good for everyone, or holding a standard that must be universally maintained, or engaging in a role reversal that puts me into someone else's shoes? Is it about the need to refrain from turning a genuine right-versus-right choice into a right-versus-wrong condemnation—by seeking to vilify one side in order that the other can look better? Or should we be talking about how to find a central pathway between two unpleasant choices? Maybe the topic should be the need to express courage, face down danger, and take action when our values

are put to the test? Or should the dialogue center on the respon-sibility to help the entire community build a long-term culture of integrity? If any one of these lights up on your mental panel, you can be pretty sure you're dealing with an ethical issue. Armed with these ideas, you'll at least know how you might start talking about it.

3. *Commitment to results.* This tool may be the most valuable because it helps bring issues to conclusion. Too often in today's world, ethics can seem like an option, a supplement, something secondary to our main purposes. Like an ornamental orange tree in a garden, it can produce handsome fruit that is essentially inedible—sour, bitter, and dry. But ethics isn't simply decorative. It's the real thing. Yes, it looks just like the ornamental shrub, but it's also productive. It's not simply a nice-sounding set of platitudes. It isn't just a list of values on the refrigerator door or an oath framed above a child's bed. No mere adornment, ethics makes things happen. It lifts aspirations, changes lives, and produces results. You can actually harvest its fruit. But it takes a commitment to do so—a will to practice, a desire to help children do things right, and a long-term investment to plant the fruit-bearing tree and help it grow to maturity.

Notice how Jim applied each of these in Deming's difficulties. It was his moral awareness that lifted him right out of his chair, plopped him into his pickup truck, and made him say to his son, "Let's go!" He knew there were significant moral issues at hand, and he wasn't about to blow right past them. Instead, he made the effort to address them head-on.

Did he have any idea how he was going to address them? Did he know what he was going to say? Probably not. But he had enough moral savvy to realize that there would be lots of openings for conversation—lots of possibilities for talking about values, thinking through dilemmas, and discussing moral courage. He trusted, in other words, that the entry points would be there when he needed them. He also had enough wisdom not to enter the conversation before it was time to do so.

Most important, he knew that he and Deming shared a commitment to make it work. No, they hadn't sat down to talk about the three lenses. But they had talked enough about ethics and values in the past to trust that each knew how much ethics mattered. They knew it was essential, not ornamental. They could trust each other to listen, respect each other's views, and want to know how the other was reasoning.

That commitment—that confidence and conviction that you can put these ideas into practice—is what this book is all about. Several years ago, a parent who had read one of our dilemmas sent back his response. After analyzing the central dilemma in all its facets, he concluded his remarks with a pithy comment. "Being a parent," he wrote, "is not for wimps!"

That's true. Ethical parenting takes moral courage, persistence, and commitment. But it brings with it a lasting fulfillment: the moral nurturing of children who know what's right, make tough choices, and stand for conscience. If parents truly help the next generation learn those qualities—not as ornaments but as practical, productive talents—there isn't a single problem facing the world that they won't find the way to address and the confidence to master.

Top Ten Tips for Ethical Parenting

These tips, distilled by my colleague Paula Mirk and Institute for Global Ethics staff through years of working with parents, children, and teachers, address two questions parents raise most frequently: "Why does ethical parenting matter?" and "What can I do to make a difference?"

Why Parenting Matters	What You Can Do
Children learn self-steerage from watching us.	Provide frequent opportunities for your children to see you as an independent thinker. Do the right thing, especially when no one's around to give you credit for it.
The language of ethics helps shape thinking and behavior.	Integrate core values into your vocabulary. Instead of encouraging kids simply to "be nice," get specific. Urge them to "be compassionate," "be respectful," "be fair."
When you think out loud, your children learn your ethics.	Let your children hear your thought monologues as evidence of how your mind works in the realm of ethics.
Your ethical reasoning elevates their critical-thinking skills.	Connect thought to action. Articulate the ethical "why" behind your behavior. Make it clear that your choices and actions are based on sound ethical reasoning.
When you stretch to do the right thing, your children grow more ethically fit.	Rather than saying, "I'm right, he's wrong," get in the habit of explaining why you and someone else disagree: "Here's how I'm thinking, and here's how he's thinking." Then be sure to ground both sides in ethics.
When you admit your own imperfections, you take the pressure off your children.	Rather than trying to seem perfect, let your children know that we all make mistakes—and take responsibility for yours.

(continued)

Why Parenting Matters	What You Can Do
If you keep your ethical aspirations high, children are likely to do the same.	Be consistent and conscientious about your ethics, and your children will more readily follow suit.
You're their number one role model.	Your behavior matters. Be conscious that your children are watching. The little things can make the biggest difference.
You promote moral courage by modeling it.	Let your children see you choose to take the tough stand over the easy way out. Talk about the challenges as you're going through them.
You make them believe in the future.	Be enthusiastic and upbeat about applying ethics in your daily life and in the future. Children look to us to paint "adulthood." What do you want them to see?

Notes

Chapter One

1. V. Talwar and K. Lee, "Development of Lying to Conceal a Transgression: Children's Control of Expressive Behaviour During Verbal Deception," *International Journal of Behavioral Development*, 2002, 26(5), 444. http://jbd.sagepub.com/cgi/content/abstract/26/5/436.

2. V. J. Rideout, U. G. Foehr, and D. F. Roberts, "Generation M²: Media in the Lives of 8- to 18-Year-Olds" (Menlo Park, Calif.: Henry J. Kaiser Family Foundation, Jan. 2010), pp. 1, 2.

3. Ibid., p. 4.

4. L. Stone, "Beyond Simple Multi-Tasking: Continuous Partial Attention," Jan. 29, 2010, http://lindastone.net/2009/11/30/beyond-simple-multi-tasking-continuous-partial-attention/.

5. F. Gino, M. I. Norton, and D. Ariely, "The Counterfeit Self: The Deceptive Costs of Faking It," *Psychological Science*, http://pss.sagepub.com/content/early/2010/03/19/0956797610366545.full.

6. R. Dawkins, *The Selfish Gene* (Oxford: Oxford University Press, 1976), p. 3.

7. M.-H. Grosbras and others, "Neural Mechanisms of Resistance to Peer Influence in Early Adolescence," *Journal of Neuroscience*, July 25, 2007, pp. 8040–8045, http://www.jneuroscience.org/cgi/content/full/27/30/8040.

8. M. Borba, *Parents Do Make a Difference: How to Raise Kids with Solid Character, Strong Minds, and Caring Hearts* (San Francisco: Jossey-Bass, 1999), pp. 101–102.

9. N. Howe and B. Strauss, *Millennials Rising: The Next Great Generation* (New York: Vintage Books, 2000).

Chapter Two

1. C. A. Nelson, M. de Haan, and K. M. Thomas, *Neuroscience of Cognitive Development: The Role of Experience and the Developing Brain* (Hoboken, N.J.: Wiley 2006), p. 138.

2. Ibid., p. 139.

3. R. M. Kidder, *Moral Courage* (New York: HarperCollins, 2005), Chapter 3.

4. Paul Bloom, "The Moral Life of Babies," *New York Times Magazine*, May 9, 2010, p. 44.

5. Boone and Crockett Club, http://www.boone-crockett.org/huntingEthics/ethics_fairchase.asp?area=huntingEthics.

6. S. Pope, *Hunting with the Bow and Arrow* (New York: Putnam, 1925), chap. 9, http://www.gutenberg.org/dirs/etext05/7hbow10.txt.

7. "A Hunter's Rule," http://www.huntingnet.com/rules.aspx.

8. R. M. Kidder, *How Good People Make Tough Choices: Resolving the Dilemmas of Ethical Living* (New York: Morrow, 1995).

9. American Academy of Pediatrics, "Early TV Viewing Habits Could Have Lasting Effect on Kids' Attention," Sept. 4, 2007, http://www.aap.org/advocacy/releases/sept07studies.htm.

10. D. Navaraez, "Triune Ethics: The Neurobiological Roots of Our Multiple Moralities," *New Ideas in Psychology*, 2008, 26(1), 95–119, http://www.nd.edu/~dnarvaez/documents/TriuneEthicsTheory0725071.pdf.

11. KidsHealth, "How TV Affects Your Child," Oct. 2008, http://kidshealth.org/parent/positive/family/tv_affects_child.html.

12. Ibid.

13. V. J. Rideout and E. Hamel, *The Media Family: Electronic Media in the Lives of Infants, Toddlers, Preschoolers and Their Parents*

(Menlo Park, Calif.: Henry J. Kaiser Family Foundation, May 2006), p. 33.

14. John F. Kennedy, "Radio and Television Report to the American People on Civil Rights," Oval Office speech, June 11, 1963. These words are inscribed on the Federal Courthouse in Boston.

Chapter Three

1. For a summary of such research, see E. A. Turner, M. Chandler, and R. W. Heffer, "The Influence of Parenting Styles, Achievement Motivation, and Self-Efficacy on Academic Performance in College Students," *Journal of College Student Development*, 2009, 50(3), 337–346.

2. L. H. Weiss and J. C. Schwarz, "The Relationship Between Parenting Types and Older Adolescents' Personality, Academic Achievement, Adjustment and Substance Use," in A. Slater and D. Muir (eds.), *The Blackwell Reader in Developmental Psychology* (Oxford: Blackwell Publishing, 1999), p. 433.

3. D. Baumrind, "Effective Parenting During the Early Adolescent Transition," in P. A. Cowan and M. Hetherington (eds.), *Family Transitions* (Mahwah, N.J.: Erlbaum Associates, 1991), p. 119.

4. Weiss and Schwarz, "The Relationship Between Parenting Types and Older Adolescents' Personality," p. 434.

5. P. J. Leman, "Authority and Moral Reasons: Parenting Style and Children's Perceptions of Adult Rule Justifications," *International Journal of Behavioral Development*, 2005, 29(4), 265–270, http://jbd.sagepub.com/cgi/reprint/29/4/265.

6. Ibid., p. 266.

7. Ibid., p. 268.

Chapter Four

1. M. D. Hauser, *Moral Minds: The Nature of Right and Wrong* (New York: HarperCollins, 2006), p. 31.

2. Virginia Military Institute, "Honor Court," http://www.vmi.edu/show.aspx?tid=36579&id=1330.

3. E-mail from Donald McCabe to the author, Jan. 22, 2010.

Chapter Five

1. B. Coloroso, *Kids Are Worth It! Giving Your Child the Gift of Inner Discipline*, rev. ed. (New York: Quill, 2002), p. 4.

2. R. M. Kidder, *Moral Courage* (New York: HarperCollins, 2005), p. 214.

3. Thomas Jefferson to Peter Carr, August 10, 1787, quoted in M. D. Hauser, *Moral Minds: The Nature of Right and Wrong* (New York: HarperCollins, 2006), p. 61.

4. R. Dawkins, *The Selfish Gene* (New York: Oxford University Press, 1976), p. 2.

5. Ibid., p. 3.

6. P. R. Amato and B. Keith, "Parental Divorce and the Well-Being of Children: A Meta-Analysis," *Psychological Bulletin*, 1991, *110*(1), 26–46.

7. R. Hughes, "The Effects of Divorce on Children," *Parenting 24/7* (University of Illinois Extension Family Life Team, Apr. 10, 2009), http://parenting247.org/article.cfm?ContentID=646.

8. P. R. Amato, "Children of Divorced Parents as Young Adults," in E. M. Hetherington (ed.), *Coping with Divorce, Single Parenting, and Remarriage: A Risk and Resiliency Perspective* (Mahwah, NJ: Erlbaum, 1999), 147–164.

9. Hughes, "The Effects of Divorce on Children."

10. Ibid., citing L. Laumann-Billings and R. E. Emery, "Distress Among Young Adults in Divorced Families," *Journal of Family Psychology*, 2000, *14*, 671–687, and J. Dunn, L. C. Davies, T. G. O'Connor, and W. Sturgess, "Family Lives and Friendships: The Perspectives of Children In Step-, Single-Parent, and Nonstep Families," *Journal of Family Psychology*, 2001, *15*, 272–287.

Chapter Six

1. D. Ariely, *Predictably Irrational: The Hidden Forces That Shape Our Decisions*, rev. and exp. ed. (New York: HarperCollins, 2009), p. 206.

2. Ibid., p. 208.

3. Ibid., p. 213.

4. A. C. Baier, *Moral Prejudices* (Cambridge, Mass.: Harvard University Press, 1991), p. 196.

5. National Stepfamily Resource Center, Auburn University, http://www.stepfamilies.info/faqs/factsheet.php.

6. Stepfamily Foundation, http://www.stepfamily.org/statistics.html.

7. C. A. Nelson, M. de Haan, and K. M. Thomas, *Neuroscience of Cognitive Development: The Role of Experience and the Developing Brain* (Hoboken, N.J.: Wiley, 2006), p. 107.

8. Ibid., p. 117.

Chapter Seven

1. J. D. Greene and others, "An fMRI Investigation of Emotional Engagement in Moral Judgment," *Science*, 2001, *293*, 2106.

2. Ibid., p. 2107.

3. Ibid.

Glossary

This glossary contains frequently used terms, followed by brief explanations of their meanings and significance. It is included to benefit readers who, as they drop into chapters and stories here and there, may encounter concepts out of their original context and may need further definitions. Because later concepts grow out of earlier ones—and because this is a short and manageable list—the terms are not listed alphabetically but in order of their appearance in the book.

————————

Values. Societies everywhere share five core moral values: honesty, responsibility, respect, fairness, and compassion. These values help us define ethics as that which is honest or truthful, responsible or accountable, respectful or tolerant, fair or equitable, and compassionate or caring—and many other synonyms are also applicable. Research to date suggests that there's no subgroup—whether determined by race, gender, ethnicity, nationality, political persuasion, economic status, or religion—that doesn't share these values. Nor are there differences by age: these values define what teens and younger children, as well as adults, think is ethical. This list of values is not in priority order; different groups may emphasize different ones at different times. You may think your daughter is not being responsible toward adults, where she feels she's being especially respectful to her friends. You both, however, believe in both those ideas—a key point of common ground for any conversation.

Unethical. This word can sound overly judgmental unless you explain that it means a departure from the five shared values. That which is unethical is that which is dishonest, irresponsible, disrespectful, unfair, or lacking in compassion. Notice the conjunction: *or*. You don't have to fail in all five categories to be unethical. Individuals who, for instance, are highly responsible, respectful, fair, and compassionate can still be dishonest—and that's enough for anyone to say, "That's unethical."

———————

Right versus wrong. Ethics is often defined as the study of right and wrong. If the core values (honesty and responsibility, for example) define what's right, their opposites (dishonesty and irresponsibility) define what's wrong. While the toughest choices we face are right versus right (where core values come in conflict with one another and we can't do both), a large group of ethical issues, especially for the youngest children, involves right versus wrong.

———————

Wrongdoing. How do we know whether the issue facing our children is about right versus wrong (a moral temptation) or about right versus right (an ethical dilemma)? If the issue is a true dilemma, both sides are right. If it's a temptation, one side is wrong. There are five quick tests for wrongdoing:

1. *Legal.* Does one side or the other break any law?
2. *Regulatory.* Does either side violate any regulations from school, club, team, or elsewhere?
3. *Stench.* Does either side instinctively smell bad?
4. *Front page.* Would you be embarrassed if what you decided to do showed up in tomorrow's newspaper?

5. *Mom.* Could you imagine your mom, or someone else you hold in high ethical regard (a favorite uncle, a coach, a mentor) doing what you're about to do?

If each side passes these tests, you're in right-versus-right territory.

———————

Right versus right. This term identifies the toughest choices, where we face true dilemmas. In such cases, each side has powerful moral arguments to support it, and yet we can't do both at the same time. In resolving such dilemmas and in helping children resolve them, it's important to remember that we're seeking the side that has the higher right. We're not trying to find out what's wrong with one side and then, by default, choosing the opposite. You cannot resolve a right-versus-right dilemma by trying to turn it into a right-versus-wrong temptation, because neither side is wrong. There are nine useful steps in resolving an ethical dilemma:

1. *Recognize that there is a moral issue.* Is this a genuinely moral question, or one merely involving manners and social conventions? Does it engage us in values that are essentially aesthetic, political, or financial rather than moral? If so, it requires an ethical decision-making model. To shunt it aside as something else will strike many people, possibly including your children, as hypocritical.

2. *Determine the actor.* If this is a moral issue, whose is it? Are you or your child the key decision maker, or does that role belong to someone else? You can still engage in ethical discussion if you're not the actor—indeed, sometimes you must do so. The question is whether you're responsible or simply involved.

3. *Gather the relevant facts.* Good decision making requires good fact finding. What actually happened here? Are we sure? Can we sift rumor and speculation from assurance and evidence?

Are you, and especially your children, sure about how the case developed, who said what to whom and when they said it, who else might have other views, and who may have played a causative role? Here the three laws of evidence are helpful: it must be accurate, complete, and relevant—or, in terms widely used in courts of law, "the truth, the whole truth, and nothing but the truth."

4. *Test for right-versus-wrong issues.* See wrongdoing.

5. *Apply the four paradigms.* See dilemma paradigms.

6. *Apply the resolution principles.* See resolution principles.

7. *Investigate trilemma options.* See trilemma.

8. *Make the decision.* Are you or your children tempted to analyze in detail but not come to a final conclusion? This failure is one of the most common reasons that dilemmas remain in limbo. It requires moral courage, a quality that, along with reason, distinguishes the endeavors of humanity from the actions of animals. Applying this step, we most fully express our true humanity.

9. *Reflect on the process.* Are you making a decision and just walking away? If so, you've short-circuited a crucial learning opportunity. Muster the courage in the coming days or weeks to revisit the decision with your children, let them draw out the lessons learned, and share with them what you gained from the process.

Dilemma paradigms. It's easy to be perplexed by ethical dilemmas, imagining that each one is new and that there are thousands of them. In fact, there are four broad patterns, or paradigms, into which our toughest choices fall:

1. *Truth versus loyalty.* This paradigm pits the needs for honest, transparent communication against the requirements for fidelity, allegiance, promise keeping, and responsibility to others.

2. *Individual versus community.* Here the powerful arguments for honoring the self (or small group) are arrayed against the equally powerful claims of the other (or large group).

3. *Short term versus long term.* The claims of immediacy and the now (which economists may see as consumption) are arrayed against the arguments for the future (or investment).

4. *Justice versus mercy.* There are sound reasons for following rules, patterns, and expectations—and sound reasons for allowing exceptions in the name of compassion and caring.

In resolving such a dilemma, imagine that you have a table in front of you with two stacks of arguments, for A and for B. These paradigms give you headings under which to develop your arguments. Even young children can quickly learn to distinguish arguments for immediate satisfaction from those for longer-term sustainability—even if "longer term" for them is tomorrow.

Resolution principles. There are numerous ways to resolve dilemmas, including bluster, inaction, tossing coins, and consulting oracles. But three have come down to us through the long traditions of moral philosophy:

1. The *ends-based* principle of utilitarianism, widely known as "doing the greatest good for the greatest number." This principle, rooted in the work of the English philosophers Jeremy Bentham and John Stuart Mill, is what philosophers describe as consequentialism. In other words, the ethics depends on the consequences, or outcomes, of your choices. If things turn out well, we did the right thing—and if they come out badly, we did the wrong thing. To follow the ends-based principle, then, requires assessing the future as carefully as possible—something none of us is very good at but is nevertheless required here. A noble principle, it is invoked by legislators who,

knowing that no piece of legislation can be totally good for everyone, try to maximize the good for the most people.

2. The *rule-based* principle, laboring under the unfortunate name of the "categorical imperative." That term, coined by German-speaking philosopher Immanuel Kant, refers to a universal law that we would want everyone to apply in similar circumstances. It calls on us to contemplate those maxims, rules, or principles that, if adhered to by everyone, would fulfill our highest moral duty. Appearing more complex than it really is, this rule-based thinking probably enters a child's world in preschool, when the teacher says, "Gosh, Johnny, if I let *you* do that, I'd have to let *everyone* do it!" Equally noble, this principle underlies the work of the judiciary, which seeks to create precedents so far-reaching and overarching that they will set universal standards for the ages and be applicable regardless of the specific description of the case or the individuals. For that reason, however, it is sometimes seen as cold and uncaring, more willing to preserve universal principles than to attend to real-time suffering.

3. The *care-based* principle of the Golden Rule. This principle, which calls on us to do to others what we would want them to do to us, is far older than the other two. Often thought to be distinctly Christian, it in fact sits at the heart of every one of the world's major religions. A principle of reciprocity, it requires us to imagine what it would be like to be the other person. In dilemmas affecting more than one other person, it can be more difficult to apply—though in practice, individuals using it usually define the "other" as someone who is known to the decision maker and in most immediate distress.

Trilemma option. This concept refers to a middle ground between two extremes, a third way out of our dilemma. The word *dilemma* derives from the Greek words *di*, meaning two, and *lemma*, meaning a fundamental proposition, an assumption taken for granted. It forces us to choose one side or the other. But sometimes the best solution lies in a compromise that extracts the best aspects from each side of the dilemma and discards the worst. Trilemma options are typically our best solutions. But not every dilemma has a trilemma option. Parents who try to force the trilemma, believing that every issue can be solved by a negotiated middle way, may become unconscionable compromisers, waffling just when they should hold their ground unflinchingly.

Moral courage. At its simplest, this term means the courage to be moral. And if being "moral" means holding to our five core values, then moral courage means the courage to be honest, responsible, respectful, fair, and compassionate. In practice, however, moral courage is best understood as the willing endurance of significant danger for the sake of principle. Those three terms—*endurance* or *stamina*, *danger* or *risk*, and *principle* or *values*—suggest that this quality depends on our commitment to what is right, our willingness to take action when our sense of right is put to the test, and our recognition that when nothing is at stake, there's no need for courage. Moral courage is the catalyst that turns values and decisions into action. Without it, parents may find that neither excellent values nor carefully calibrated moral reasoning will, by themselves, have any impact or create any change.

Further Reading

Ariely, D. *Predictably Irrational: The Hidden Forces That Shape Our Decisions.* (Rev. and exp. ed.) New York: HarperCollins, 2009.

Borba, M. *Parents Do Make a Difference: How to Raise Kids with Solid Character, Strong Minds, and Caring Hearts.* San Francisco: Jossey-Bass, 1999.

Borba, M. *Building Moral Intelligence: The Seven Essential Virtues That Teach Kids to Do the Right Thing.* San Francisco: Jossey-Bass, 2001.

Coles, R. *The Moral Intelligence of Children: How to Raise a Moral Child.* New York: Random House, 1997.

Coloroso, B. *Kids Are Worth It! Giving Your Child the Gift of Inner Discipline.* (Rev. ed.) New York: Quill, 2002.

Coloroso, B. *Just Because It's Not Wrong Doesn't Make It Right: Teaching Kids to Think and Act Ethically.* New York: Penguin, 2005.

Faber, A., and Mazlish, E. *How to Talk So Kids Will Listen and Listen So Kids Will Talk.* New York: Avon, 1980.

Hauser, M. D. *Moral Minds: The Nature of Right and Wrong.* New York: HarperCollins, 2006.

Kidder, R. M. *Moral Courage.* New York: HarperCollins, 2005.

Kidder, R. M. *How Good People Make Tough Choices: Resolving the Dilemmas of Ethical Living.* (Rev. ed.) New York: HarperCollins, 2009.

Paren, E. *Surgically Shaping Children: Technology, Ethics, and the Pursuit of Normality.* Baltimore, Md.: Johns Hopkins University Press, 2006.

Shalit, W. *Girls Gone Mild: Young Women Reclaim Self-Respect and Find It's Not Bad to Be Good.* New York: Random House, 2007.

About the Author

Rushworth M. Kidder is founder and president of the Institute for Global Ethics, a nonprofit organization established in 1990 that promotes character and integrity in corporations, government agencies, schools, and professional groups. He was previously foreign correspondent, senior columnist, and feature editor for the *Christian Science Monitor,* and he has been a regular contributor to *Oprah* magazine on ethics questions. The author of ten books on subjects ranging from international ethics to the global future, he won the 1980 Explicator Literary Foundation Award for his book on the poetry of e. e. cummings. He is a trustee of the Charles Stewart Mott Foundation and serves on the advisory board of *Religion and Ethics Newsweekly* on public television. A graduate of Amherst College, he holds a Ph.D. in English and American literature from Columbia University.

Questions for Discussion

If you want to think about the issues raised in this book and apply them to your own life, consider the questions below, which are organized by chapter. I hope they'll be useful and stimulating for you on your own, or perhaps in a book reading club or other literary or educational setting.

There are no right or wrong answers, just an opportunity to think about these choices and discuss them with others.

Chapter One

Read "Controlling the Influence of Electronic Media." Surveys find that eight to eighteen year olds absorb more than seven and a half hours of media content every day. Much of this time they are multitasking, leading to what researcher Linda Stone describes as "continuous partial attention."

1. Have you seen evidence of continuous partial attention in your children's lives? If so, does it cause you to marvel at their ability to juggle multiple inputs, or worry about their inability to focus?

2. Is continuous partial attention an important new coping skill that young people need in a complex world? Or is it an addictive tendency we should help children overcome?

"Helping Children Be Real in a World of Fakes" reports that college students who knowingly wore counterfeit sunglasses during an experiment were more than twice as likely to cheat as those wearing authentic sunglasses. Researchers concluded that wearing counterfeits signals "an aspiration to be something one is not," generating in those wearers "a feeling of a 'counterfeit self' that leads them to behave unethically."

1. Have you bought fake products? Have you seen in others, or experienced in yourself, a "feeling of a 'counterfeit self'" because of their use? What were your feelings about this experience?

2. Is interest in buying knockoffs, look-alikes, and other bogus inexpensive products an innocent activity or a serious problem in today's culture? Should it be accepted as one way for individuals of modest means to maintain an up-to-date look and feel good about their appearance? Or should it be resisted as a damaging behavior that promotes counterfeit selfhood?

3. If your children raise the issue of buying phony designer items, what will you say?

Chapter Two

Read "Branson and the Gold Coins," which recounts a mother's story of her three-year-old son who lifted some foil-wrapped chocolate coins from a store. When she recognized what her son had done, she had to decide how—and whether—to correct his behavior.

1. Have you faced a situation with your children that clearly involved right and wrong yet made you ask, "Am I making a mountain out of molehill? Am I overreacting?" Describe the situation and how it made you feel.

2. Are some ethical issues too insignificant to worry about at any given moment? In your own life, how do you draw the line between insignificance and importance?

Read "Loren Wrecks the Train," which tells of a two year old who loves trains, builds them with his interlocking-block set, and delights in pushing them into colossal wrecks. His mother, who lets him watch television sparingly, is concerned that his appetite for violent and spectacular accidents is whetted by the programs he watches.

1. Many stories, from fairy tales to children's television programs, use violence to heighten the dramatic effect. Can you think of ways in which your child, through television or other means, may be inadvertently learning that violence is interesting and fun?

2. With the development of special effects in films and video, it's difficult to avoid spectacular scenes in visual media. Are you worried about the influence of this realistic sensational violence on your child? Or do you think the experience of watching such visual stimulation has no actual connection to a child's behavior in the real world?

3. If you had to explain to a preschooler what's wrong with creating pretend accidents and wrecks while he or she is playing, what would you say? Is such play a good outlet for letting off steam?

Chapter Three

Read "Teaching Thrift in an Age of Opulence" about Chrissie's desire to help her eight-year-old daughter learn the value of frugality.

1. Researcher Diana Baumrind, categorizing parenting styles based on "demandingness" and "responsiveness," notes that some parents are overly permissive, while others are too authoritarian. Think about other parents you know. Do you think that on the whole, they tend to be too permissive? Too authoritarian? Balanced about right?

2. How would you categorize the parenting you received as a youth: too permissive, too authoritarian, or balanced? In general, do you think that parents today are more permissive or more authoritarian than parents were when you were growing up? If so, what influences have caused these changes? If not, what influences have maintained stability?

3. Consider the questions toward the end of the chapter that begin, "Did Will [Chrissie's father] wisely surrender? Or was this a cowardly capitulation?" In this story, did Will get the balance right, or did he slide too far in one direction?

4. As you consider your own parenting style, which side (too permissive or too authoritarian) do you worry you might slide into if you aren't careful? What are you doing to avoid that slide?

Read "Teaching Ethics Through Principles." Here, Daphne shares an embarrassing secret about a classmate during a party game. She learns the importance of speaking, as well as acting, on the basis of her five core values of honesty, respect, responsibility, fairness, and compassion.

1. Did Grant and Holly respond correctly to their daughter, Daphne? Should they have made stronger demands on her? Or did they overreact? Why do you think this?

2. Reconsidering your own experiences as a parent, which of these five core values do you think comes most easily to your children and requires the least explanation? Which do you think is the hardest for them to understand and practice? Why do you think that's so?

3. Thinking about the behavior of your children, which of these five values is most at risk in the behavior of their peer group and most in need of constant attention? How can you help them strengthen that value?

Chapter Four

In "Resolving Ethical Dilemmas," Lara faces a right-versus-right dilemma about whether to tell the teachers at her son's new school that he has had problems with attention deficit disorder (ADD), though he no longer needs medication.

1. Lara decided not to tell the school. Did she make the right choice? Why or why not?

2. Think of an occasion when you've had a tough right-versus-right choice. Working with your group, apply the four dilemma paradigms to it. Which seems to fit the best? How does this process help you make a better choice?

3. Working with your group, apply the three resolution principles. Which seems to fit the best?

4. Within your group, did you all come to the same conclusion about what was right? Did everyone favor the same method, or did different individuals favor different methods? If good people can use differing routes to arrive at different moral conclusions, what constitutes sound moral judgment?

In "Zero Tolerance," fourteen-year-old Chase gets caught drinking at his school, which has a strict no-drinking policy. The assistant headmaster, John, calls the parents to explain—and finds himself in a complicated situation.

1. If you were Chase's mom, Tally, how would you respond to John's call? Would you tell him about your son's prior drinking experience? Why or why not?

2. Is John facing a right-versus-right dilemma, or is this simply a right-versus-wrong infraction?

3. Do you think Chase should be expelled? Why or why not?

4. Based on this discussion, do you think you should talk to your children about school policies on drinking? If so, what are the most effective arguments to make, one way or another?

Chapter Five

Read "Finding the Third Way," where a father uses storytelling to raise an ethical question with college-age children.

1. To make his point, Charlie passed off a fiction as though it were a fact. Is it okay to lie to make an ethical point? Or was Charlie not really lying?

2. Recall a time when you had a serious conversation about an ethical issue with a teenage child. Can you think of a story you could have invented or a true story from the past you might have used instead? Was the invented story more effective than a true one would have been?

3. The trilemma option finds a middle ground between two unpleasant alternatives. What's the difference between finding a third way and ducking a tough decision?

In "A Sexual Crisis," Cort finds a way to have a needed conversation with his daughter's boyfriend about sexual issues—an uncomfortable conversation he doesn't really want to have.

1. Is Cort expressing moral courage, or is he just being officious and butting in when he shouldn't? Why or why not? How do you distinguish these two conditions?

2. Think of an occasion when you needed to raise an uncomfortable ethical issue with a child. What gave you the courage to do so? What did you learn from the encounter? What did the child learn?

Chapter Six

Read "Counseling, Not Controlling." Summarizing his research on dishonest behavior among college students, Daniel Ariely concludes that "when we are removed from any benchmarks of ethical thought, we tend to stray into dishonesty. But if we are reminded of morality at the moment we are tempted, then we are much more likely to be honest."

1. Why do you think being reminded of "benchmarks of ethical thought" promotes honesty?

2. Do you see evidence in today's culture of unethical benchmarks that remind us of immorality? Do you think those negative benchmarks encourage dishonesty? Why or why not?

3. What does the word *platitude* mean to you? How do you distinguish a platitude from a "benchmark of ethical thought"?

4. In this story, Cynthia worried that when she reminded David of such benchmarks, he might see her as spouting platitudes. What would you say to Cynthia to help her spot the difference between useful benchmarks and mere platitudes?

Read "Supporting Your Daughter or Saving Your Grandchildren." In this example, Fran and her husband face a stark choice concerning their drug-using daughter who lives in their home with her two children. "Should they banish Alice from the only home she had in order to protect their grandchildren from their mother's influence? Or should they continue trying to nurture and sustain their daughter at the risk of harming Tina, now nine years old, and her sister?"

1. Think of as many arguments as possible for banishing Alice from the house. Then think of all the arguments for keeping her in the house.

2. Which argument makes the most sense to you? If you were Fran, what would you do?

3. Which choice—to banish or to nurture—requires more moral courage? Why? Do you think the right choice is always the one requiring the most moral courage?

Chapter Seven

The story of Jim and his son, Deming, addresses the role of emotion in moral judgment.

1. There are several actors in this story. Which of them had the most moral courage? Who had the least?

2. Take a few minutes to fill in Figure 7.1 with examples from your own experience. First, think of a parenting dilemma that was *personal* but not *moral* (lower right quadrant). Now think of one that was *moral* but not *personal* (upper left quadrant). Then fill in the other two quadrants.

3. Of your four examples, which one do you feel is the most difficult to resolve? Which takes the most courage? Which evokes the greatest emotion? Are emotional dilemmas always the ones that require the most courage and present the hardest choices, or is emotion not a factor in determining the courage that's required or the difficulty of the decision?

4. How should we manage the emotional content of our dilemmas? Should we strive to be entirely unemotional as parents, signaling to our children the importance of impersonal rationality? Or should we be willing to show our emotions at every turn, signaling how much we care? In this story, what did Jim do to strike the right balance? How can you strike the right balance?

Look for other stories in this book that raise questions that interest you and apply to your life. And if you have any more questions or ideas about them you'd like me to respond to, my e-mail is rkidder@globalethics.org.

Index